Twisted steel, chunks of concrete and charred trees are all that remain of a once-busy shopping district in Hiroshima on the 7th of August, 1945—the day after the atomic bomb was dropped. The cataclysmic blast, and a similar one three days later at Nagasaki, almost immediately claimed some 200,000 lives and convinced Japanese leaders of the futility of continuing the War.

THE FALL OF JAPAN

Other Publications:
PLANET EARTH
COLLECTOR'S LIBRARY OF THE CIVIL WAR
LIBRARY OF HEALTH
CLASSICS OF THE OLD WEST
THE EPIC OF FLIGHT
THE GOOD COOK
THE SEAFARERS
THE ENCYCLOPEDIA OF COLLECTIBLES
THE GREAT CITIES
HOME REPAIR AND IMPROVEMENT
THE WORLD'S WILD PLACES
THE TIME-LIFE LIBRARY OF BOATING
HUMAN BEHAVIOR
THE ART OF SEWING
THE OLD WEST
THE EMERGENCE OF MAN
THE AMERICAN WILDERNESS
THE TIME-LIFE ENCYCLOPEDIA OF GARDENING
LIFE LIBRARY OF PHOTOGRAPHY
THIS FABULOUS CENTURY
FOODS OF THE WORLD
TIME-LIFE LIBRARY OF AMERICA
TIME-LIFE LIBRARY OF ART
GREAT AGES OF MAN
LIFE SCIENCE LIBRARY
THE LIFE HISTORY OF THE UNITED STATES
TIME READING PROGRAM
LIFE NATURE LIBRARY
LIFE WORLD LIBRARY
FAMILY LIBRARY:
    HOW THINGS WORK IN YOUR HOME
    THE TIME-LIFE BOOK OF THE FAMILY CAR
    THE TIME-LIFE FAMILY LEGAL GUIDE
    THE TIME-LIFE BOOK OF FAMILY FINANCE

This volume is one of a series that chronicles
in full the events of the Second World War.
Previous books in the series include:

Prelude to War   Road to Tokyo
Blitzkrieg   Red Army Resurgent
The Battle of Britain   The Nazis
The Rising Sun   Across the Rhine
The Battle of the Atlantic War under the Pacific
Russia Besieged   War in the Outposts
The War in the Desert   The Soviet Juggernaut
The Home Front: U.S.A.   Japan at War
China-Burma-India   The Mediterranean
Island Fighting   Battles for Scandinavia
The Italian Campaign   The Secret War
Partisans and Guerrillas   Prisoners of War
The Second Front   The Commandos
Liberation   The Home Front: Germany
Return to the Philippines   Italy at War
The Air War in Europe   Bombers over Japan
The Resistance   The Neutrals
The Battle of the Bulge   Victory in Europe

WORLD WAR II · TIME-LIFE BOOKS · ALEXANDRIA, VIRGINIA

BY KEITH WHEELER
AND THE EDITORS OF TIME-LIFE BOOKS

THE FALL OF JAPAN

Time-Life Books Inc.
is a wholly owned subsidiary of
TIME INCORPORATED

Founder: Henry R. Luce 1898-1967

Editor-in-Chief: Henry Anatole Grunwald
President: J. Richard Munro
Chairman of the Board: Ralph P. Davidson
Executive Vice President: Clifford J. Grum
Editorial Director: Ralph Graves
Group Vice President, Books: Joan D. Manley
Vice Chairman: Arthur Temple

TIME-LIFE BOOKS INC.

Editor: George Constable
Executive Editor: George Daniels
Director of Design: Louis Klein
Board of Editors: Dale M. Brown, Thomas H. Flaherty
Jr., Thomas A. Lewis, Martin Mann, Robert G. Mason,
John Paul Porter, Gerry Schremp, Gerald Simons,
Rosalind Stubenberg, Kit van Tulleken
Director of Administration: David L. Harrison
Director of Research: Carolyn L. Sackett
Director of Photography: Richard Kenin

President: Reginald K. Brack Jr.
Executive Vice Presidents: John Steven Maxwell,
David J. Walsh
Vice Presidents: George Artandi, Stephen L. Bair,
Peter G. Barnes, Nicholas Benton, John L. Canova,
Beatrice T. Dobie, James L. Mercer, Paul R. Stewart

WORLD WAR II

Editor: Thomas H. Flaherty Jr.
Senior Editor: Henry Woodhead
Designer: Van W. Carney
Chief Researcher: Philip Brandt George

Editorial Staff for The Fall of Japan
Associate Editor: Jeremy Ross
Text Editors: Richard D. Kovar, Robert Menaker
Staff Writers: Donald Davison Cantlay,
Paul N. Mathless
Researchers: Scarlet Cheng, Ann Dusel Corson,
Reginald H. Dickerson, Margaret Gray, Trudy W.
Pearson, Alfreda Robertson, Marta Ann Sanchez
Copy Coordinators: Ann Bartunek, Allan Fallow,
Elizabeth Graham, Barbara F. Quarmby
Art Assistant: Mikio Togashi
Picture Coordinator: Renée DeSandies
Editorial Assistant: Andrea E. Reynolds

Special Contributors:
Keiko Foster, Martha Reichard George

Editorial Operations
Design: Arnold C. Holeywell (assistant director);
Anne B. Landry (art coordinator); James J. Cox
(quality control)
Research: Jane Edwin (assistant director),
Louise D. Forstall
Copy Room: Susan Galloway Goldberg (director),
Celia Beattie, Ricki Tarlow
Production: Feliciano Madrid (director),
Gordon E. Buck, Peter Inchautequiz

Correspondents: Elisabeth Kraemer (Bonn); Margot
Hapgood, Dorothy Bacon (London); Miriam Hsia,
Lucy T. Voulgaris (New York); Maria Vincenza Aloisi,
Josephine du Brusle (Paris); Ann Natanson (Rome).
Valuable assistance was also provided by: Janet Zich
(Half Moon Bay, California); Felix Rosenthal
(Moscow); Christina Lieberman (New York); Kazuo
Ohyauchi (Tokyo).

The Author: KEITH WHEELER, a South Dakota newspaperman and a writer for Life, covered the War against Japan as a correspondent for the Chicago Daily Times and wrote of his experiences in The Pacific Is My Beat and We Are the Wounded. He has published a number of novels and nonfiction books and contributed five volumes to the Time-Life Books Old West series. He is the author of three previous volumes in the World War II series: The Road to Tokyo, War under the Pacific and Bombers over Japan.

The Consultants: COLONEL JOHN R. ELTING, USA (Ret.), a military historian, is the author of The Battle of Bunker's Hill, The Battles of Saratoga and Military History and Atlas of the Napoleonic Wars. He is the editor of Military Uniforms in America, a historical series now in its third volume, and was associate editor of The West Point Atlas of American Wars.

RICHARD BAKER is a chemist and metallurgist who began work on the Manhattan Project's plutonium bomb at Los Alamos, New Mexico, in 1943, and has worked there ever since. In 1981 he retired as Associate Director for National Security Programs at the Los Alamos National Laboratory and now serves as a consultant to the Director of the Laboratory.

JACOB BESER interrupted his engineering studies at Johns Hopkins University after Pearl Harbor to serve in the U.S. Army Air Forces as a radar countermeasures officer; he flew on both the Hiroshima and the Nagasaki atomic strike missions. Since the end of World War II he has lectured widely on the role of nuclear weapons in the defeat of Japan.

NATHANIEL THAYER is Director of Asian Studies at the Johns Hopkins University School of Advanced International Studies in Washington, D.C.; he served in Japan and the Far East with the U.S. Army, the Department of State, and as a consultant to the U.S. and Japanese governments. He is the author of How the Conservatives Rule Japan and a number of works on East Asia.

Library of Congress Cataloguing in Publication Data

Wheeler, Keith.
    Fall of Japan.

    (World War II; v. 37)
    Bibliography: p.
    Includes index.
    1. World War, 1939-1945—Japan. 2. Atomic bomb.
3. Hiroshima-ken (Japan)—Bombardment, 1945.
4. Nagasaki-shi (Japan)—Bombardment, 1945.
5. Japan—History—1912-1945.   I. Time-Life
Books.   II. Title.   III. Series.
D767.2.W48   940.54′26   82-5754
ISBN 0-8094-3409-1   AACR2
ISBN 0-8094-3408-3 (lib. bdg.)
ISBN 0-8094-3407-5 (retail ed.)

For information about any Time-Life book, please write:

Reader Information
Time-Life Books
541 North Fairbanks Court
Chicago, Illinois 60611

© 1983 Time-Life Books Inc. All rights reserved.
No part of this book may be reproduced in any form or by any
electronic or mechanical means, including information storage and retrieval devices or systems, without prior written permission from the publisher, except that brief passages may be
quoted for reviews.
First printing. Printed in U.S.A.
Published simultaneously in Canada.
School and library distribution by Silver Burdett Company,
Morristown, New Jersey.

TIME-LIFE is a trademark of Time Incorporated U.S.A.

CONTENTS

...remem...
I'm s...

SPECTER OF A HALF-WON WAR

Lusting for combat, a Japanese officer strokes his sword in a U.S. propaganda poster recalling past battles and reminding Americans that the War rages on.

ROUSING THE NATION FOR THE FINAL DRIVE

Sighting down his rifle, a tough-looking Japanese soldier takes aim in this U.S. Army poster issued as a reminder that one dangerous foe remained.

Germany had been knocked out of the War, and now the United States turned with a vengeance against Japan. In the spring and early summer of 1945, a torrent of American planes, ships and fighting men began to flow into the Pacific theater, which by command decision had taken a back seat to victory in Europe.

An old battle cry—"Remember Pearl Harbor!"—sounded with renewed urgency. But Americans, remembering not only Pearl Harbor but Guadalcanal, Saipan, Palau and a dozen other brutal encounters, expected that the final victory would come hard.

As long as Japan continued to fight, the War was only half over—and the second half was growing ever more costly as United States forces drew nearer and nearer to the Japanese home islands. Posters like those displayed here and on the following pages were part of a nationwide campaign to keep America's patriotic spirits and production levels high. Even before V-E Day, posters appeared showing Uncle Sam rolling up his sleeves and issuing the flinty challenge: "Jap . . . You're Next!"

Though the Japanese were everywhere in retreat, the poster campaign dwelled less on recent victories than on the early defeats and traumatic standoffs. These were experiences that rankled Americans—and spurred them to work harder. Private industry added its own exhortations to the posters that were commissioned by the government. One series developed by the Douglas Aircraft Company featured the Tokio Kid, a cartoon Japanese soldier *(page 13)* who promoted a repertoire of wartime vices, offering instruction to American factory workers in clock watching, carelessness and waste.

But the emotion most frequently appealed to was not guilt over sloppy work habits but revenge—anger directed at a savage and still-dangerous enemy who appeared in various caricatures as the Sneaky Jap, the Brutal Jap, the Tenacious Jap. Clearly, with such a foe at large, this was no time to relax—no matter how devoutly Americans wanted the great conflict to be over.

Having subdued one enemy, a muscular Uncle Sam turns his attention to Japan in a bond-drive poster by James Montgomery Flagg.

PLEAS FROM THE MEN IN UNIFORM

American fighting men—including Admiral Chester W. Nimitz (near right)—call on the home front for help to carry the War to Tokyo and thus avenge Pearl Harbor. At bottom right, a blinded GI reminds both soldiers and civilians to take the enemy seriously.

PLEAS FROM THE MEN IN UNIFORM

The Japanese are presented as grinning stereotypes speaking pidgin English in posters aimed at workers in American war industries. Above, a smirking general thanks absentees at Chrysler, a leading manufacturer of tanks, and a bucktoothed Japan takes it on the chin in the "Battle for Production." The posters opposite are from a series produced by Douglas Aircraft and feature, in various guises, a subversive character named the Tokio Kid.

A home in ruins and a pleading child (above) warn Americans that their shores are not yet safe. In two other posters, a phalanx of citizens (right), representing 85 million Americans who invested in War bonds, marches in support of the final bond drive, while the nation's industrial muscle (far right) is symbolized by a woman—fittingly so, since females now constituted one third of the work force.

1

The end of the war in Asia seemed tantalizingly close by the summer of 1945. After three years of crushing defeats, Japan no longer possessed the means to wage offensive warfare. All of its strategic island bastions in the Pacific had been captured or neutralized by the Allies, at great cost in blood and lives. Japan's Navy and its air arm had been shattered in the Battles of the Philippine Sea and Leyte Gulf, and in the futile defense of Okinawa and Iwo Jima. The Japanese home islands were being devastated; Major General Curtis E. LeMay's XXI Bomber Command, operating from bases in the newly won Marianas, had fire-bombed vast sections of major Japanese cities into charred ruin.

By the end of June, the incendiary attacks had destroyed 2.5 million houses and had left 13 million Japanese homeless. Moreover, a U.S. naval blockade had severed Japan's life lines to the outside world. No longer could the island nation rely on imports of fuel, food and raw materials from its conquests in China, Korea and Manchuria. Packs of American submarines roamed Japanese waters with impunity, sinking freighters and tankers that tried to run the blockade; Allied battleships and cruisers intruded within gun range of the Japanese shores, shelling port installations and military compounds. Carrier-based fighters and bombers swarmed over the islands, seeking targets of opportunity: railway tracks and trains, motorized troop convoys, factories and airfields.

Japan was starving. The homeless picked through the rubble of their ravaged cities or made their way into the countryside to dig sustenance from the nearly barren fields. A measure of the government's desperation came in July, when it issued a decree urging the people to collect acorns, perhaps the only food that still existed in abundance.

Yet even in this season of despair, the Japanese gave no concrete signs of capitulating. Their reluctance to lay down arms stemmed both from their rigid code of honor—to surrender was a disgrace—and from their concern for the future of Emperor Hirohito, whom they venerated as a descendant of the gods. The Japanese leadership feared the worst for Hirohito should the country surrender; conceivably, he could be tried as a war criminal and imprisoned or even executed. Almost as intolerable, Hirohito's imperial dynasty might be abolished by the conquerors and another form of government instituted by force.

A RACE TO HARNESS THE ATOM

All of these possibilities were abhorrent to the Japanese, and rather than expose Hirohito to indignity or harm, they were prepared to sacrifice their nation. Grimly, Japanese military strategists laid plans for a last-ditch defense of the home islands in case of an Allied invasion. The plans called for all able-bodied men, women and children to arm themselves with knives and bamboo spears and to join the home guard in repulsing the invaders on the beaches. As the Japanese well knew, this was a blueprint for national suicide.

An invasion of Japan was an equally grim prospect for Allied leaders as they pondered alternatives for ending the War. American military chiefs were divided on the issue. Several of them, including General LeMay, argued against an invasion; they maintained that Japan could not survive the combined effects of the naval blockade and continued aerial attacks. "We could bomb and burn them until they quit," LeMay asserted. But a majority of the Joint Chiefs, including U.S. Army Chief of Staff General George C. Marshall, disagreed.

To the Marshall faction, time was crucial. Now that Germany had surrendered, Americans felt a new sense of urgency to end the fighting and bring the servicemen home. Most of the Joint Chiefs believed that Japan was capable of fighting on well into 1946. They reached the somber conclusion that only a massive invasion would force Japan to surrender within a reasonable length of time. The new American President, Harry S. Truman, accepted their decision. But, like the Joint Chiefs, Truman was appalled at the estimates of casualties from such an invasion: As many as one million Americans and at least that many Japanese would be killed or wounded.

The Allies planned to invade Kyushu, Japan's southernmost major island, at the beginning of November 1945; Kyushu would be secured as a staging area for a final assault on Honshu, the principal island in the Japanese chain (page 18). Most American military leaders viewed this strategy as inevitable; there were only a few among them who knew of another plan for ending the War, a solution dazzlingly simple in concept, yet awesomely complex in execution. These men were privy to one of history's great secrets: For two years, hundreds of thousands of Americans had been laboring at far-flung installations to produce the ultimate weapon, a fantastically powerful bomb, from atomic energy.

This stupendous project, the most ambitious and costly scientific endeavor ever conceived by the mind of man, marshaled the genius of nuclear physicists, the resources of giant industry and the ingenuity of obscure craftsmen. All but a select few of the thousands involved worked in ignorance of the common goal: the creation of an atomic bomb. Their success in the summer of 1945 constituted an unparalleled technological achievement. For the unsuspecting Japanese, it triggered a holocaustal nightmare of suffering and death. For the world, it brought peace—and the dawn of a perilous postwar era called the Atomic Age.

The chain of events that led to the creation of the bomb began with scientific experiments conducted during the 1930s. Physicists in the United States and on the Continent were bombarding a variety of natural elements with streams of neutrons to discover how the atomic structure of matter might be transformed. Uranium, nature's heaviest element, seemed the most promising target. On December 8, 1938, two scientists bombarding uranium at the Kaiser Wilhelm Institute in Berlin succeeded in accomplishing something extraordinary: They split the nucleus of an atom.

The German physicists, Otto Hahn and Fritz Strassmann, reported their findings to a former colleague, Lise Meitner, who was by then a refugee from Nazism in Sweden. Meitner and a visiting nephew, Otto Frisch, analyzed the Berliners' experiments and repeated them with the same results. Back in his own laboratory in Denmark shortly after Christmas, Frisch bettered the feat. He not only split an atom but also measured a minuscule release of energy.

Frisch confided in Niels Bohr, the Nobel Prize-winning Danish physicist, who was about to sail for the United States to lecture at Princeton University. Soon after Bohr arrived, he shared his information, in dramatic fashion, with the American scientific community. On January 26, 1939, he delivered a detailed account of the atom-splitting experiments to a gathering of approximately 50 physicists in Washington, D.C. Bohr's report threw the conference of staid and serious scientists into an uproar. Many of them realized that they were on the verge of a similar breakthrough in nuclear experimentation.

Bohr's report was so explicit that a group of physicists from Johns Hopkins University in nearby Baltimore hurried

THE TWO-STEP PLAN TO INVADE JAPAN

To crush Japan into submission, the U.S. Joint Chiefs envisioned a massive two-stage invasion of the Empire's home islands involving some five million troops, most of them American. The first stage, named Operation *Olympic*, was scheduled for November 1945. It called for one corps of the U.S. Sixth Army to feint toward Shikoku island, while three other corps landed on Kyushu, the southernmost main island, and converged on Kagoshima Bay, the primary objective.

Once open to Allied shipping, the 50-mile-wide bay would be a staging area for the invasion's second phase, Operation *Coronet*. Planned for March 1946, *Coronet* was aimed at Honshu, Japan's largest island and its industrial and governmental heart. The U.S. Eighth Army would land at Sagami Bay and thrust west and north to take Yokohama, Kumagaya and Koga. The First Army, meanwhile, would go ashore on the Kwanto plain and attack westward to capture Tokyo and force the surrender.

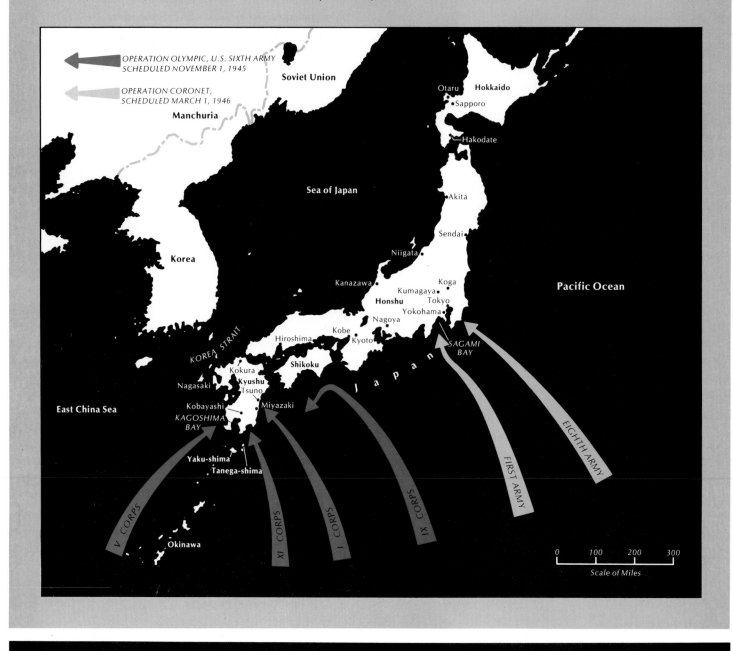

home to their laboratory and split a uranium nucleus before sundown. That night the procedure was duplicated at the Carnegie Institution in Washington. Within days, particle accelerators at the University of Chicago and the University of California at Berkeley were bombarding uranium with neutrons, and the pulsing green lines on attached oscilloscopes were measuring the minute bursts of energy. "The Department of Physics at Princeton was like a stirred ant heap," said Leo Szilard, a refugee Hungarian physicist then in residence at the New Jersey university.

Szilard was one of a number of émigré European scientists who had recently arrived in the United States as fugitives from Nazism and Fascism. They included Szilard's fellow Hungarians Edward Teller and Eugene Wigner, the Italian Enrico Fermi, the German Hans Bethe and others. Like their American colleagues, they were enthralled by the discovery of fission.

No one was more excited than Szilard. Nearly five years earlier he had postulated that if the atom could be split by hammering it with neutrons, it would in turn release more neutrons, which under certain conditions would split the nuclei of other atoms. The result would be a self-sustaining chain reaction and the release of untold energy.

Szilard went to work to prove his theory, and by March of 1939 he and a colleague, working at Columbia University, succeeded in producing a laboratory-scale chain reaction using uranium. Exultantly he telephoned his friend Edward Teller in Washington. "I have found the neutrons," he said in excited Hungarian. Teller understood. The creation of a controlled chain reaction meant that nuclear power—and an atomic weapon—was now theoretically possible. Szilard was perhaps the first to recognize the ominous side of his success. "That night," he said, "I knew the world was headed for sorrow."

In the spring of 1939, Niels Bohr, working at Princeton with a young American physicist, John Wheeler, made another major contribution to nuclear knowledge. The two men demonstrated that only a minute quantity of natural uranium, or U-238, was fissionable. This was an isotope they called U-235, which made up less than 1 per cent of the natural ore. If there were some way to separate U-235 from U-238 in large enough quantities, the isotope could be used to create a mighty explosion. To Bohr, such an explosion seemed beyond human reach. "It can never be done," he told Edward Teller, "unless you turn the whole United States into one huge factory."

Experiments in 1940 at the Berkeley laboratories revealed another odd characteristic of uranium, which was turning out to be a most mysterious element. Under certain conditions of neutron bombardment, part of U-238 would be transformed briefly into an entirely new element, which the experimenters named neptunium. Further processing would transform this new isotope into still another element. It was called plutonium, and it was eminently fissionable.

Now the nuclear scientists possessed the raw materials and the crude process for creating the most powerful energy source ever conceived by mankind: U-235 or plutonium set loose in an instantaneous chain reaction. Behind their startling discoveries lay a burning moral question: What should they do with their potent new knowledge? The scientists' answer to the question was dictated by concern that an enemy might develop the bomb first.

From the start, the scientific community in the United States had been acutely aware that the original breakthrough in nuclear research had occurred in a laboratory in Berlin. The refugee scientists, in particular, harbored both enormous respect for German science and a deep-rooted dread of Adolf Hitler. Their fears were dramatically confirmed in March 1939, when the Nazis seized Czechoslovakia and then banned the export of that country's uranium ores.

During the summer of 1939 these forebodings prompted the scientists to try to alert the U.S. government to the peril of nuclear fission in Hitler's hands. Both Fermi and Szilard approached the Navy—with little result except to stir some modest interest in nuclear energy as a possible source of power for submarines.

In midsummer, Szilard and Eugene Wigner called on another refugee scientist, Albert Einstein, at his summer retreat on Long Island. They knew that the renowned, white-haired father of modern physics was a friend of Belgium's Queen Elizabeth, and they hoped he might be persuaded to warn her about possible German attempts to get control of the rich uranium deposits in the Belgian Congo.

Einstein agreed to alert the Queen, but then Szilard, a man of dynamic and domineering temperament, was struck by a better idea. Frustrated by his failure to spark government interest, Szilard decided that the way to reach the top was to start at the top. If any name in science would command attention, he reasoned, it was that of Einstein.

The result was a letter addressed to "F. D. Roosevelt, President of the United States" and signed, "Yours very truly, Albert Einstein."

The letter was delayed in transit. On September 1, 1939, Hitler's legions struck Poland; two days later France and England declared war. In the ensuing crisis, Roosevelt was unreachable until October 11. On that day the missive was hand-delivered to him by Alexander Sachs, a New York banker who was both a personal friend of FDR's and a confidant of the nuclear physicist's. The President studied the letter, which described the development of nuclear chain reactions that would generate vast amounts of power and warned of the consequences:

> *This new phenomenon would also lead to the construction of bombs, and it is conceivable— though much less certain—that extremely powerful bombs of a new type may thus be constructed. A single bomb of this type, carried by boat and exploded in a port, might very well destroy the whole port together with some of the surrounding territory. However, such bombs might very well prove to be too heavy for transport by air. . . .*

Roosevelt finished reading and turned to Sachs. "Alex," he said, "what you are after is to see that the Nazis don't blow us up." The President handed the letter to Brigadier General Edwin M. Watson, his military aide, and said, "This requires action." The action ultimately taken moved the gentle Einstein, years later, to remark: "I made one great mistake in my life, when I signed the letter to President Roosevelt."

In spite of the President's directive, the U.S. government's inquiry into the uses of atomic energy began very slowly. A Uranium Committee, appointed at Roosevelt's behest, convened promptly but agreed on nothing except that building an atomic bomb was merely a possibility—and a very remote possibility at that. Thereafter the program slipped into a morass of bureaucratic indecision, and remained mired for more than a year.

The committee members did not share the urgency felt by the refugee scientists, who dreaded what might already be taking place in nuclear laboratories controlled by the Nazis. The United States, after all, was at peace. Congress was reluctant to spend money on arcane weaponry, and the development of an atomic weapon was an uncharted venture certain to cost a great deal.

The first public money the Uranium Committee spent was a grant of $6,000 to Columbia University to finance Enrico Fermi in modest experiments with graphite and uranium ox-

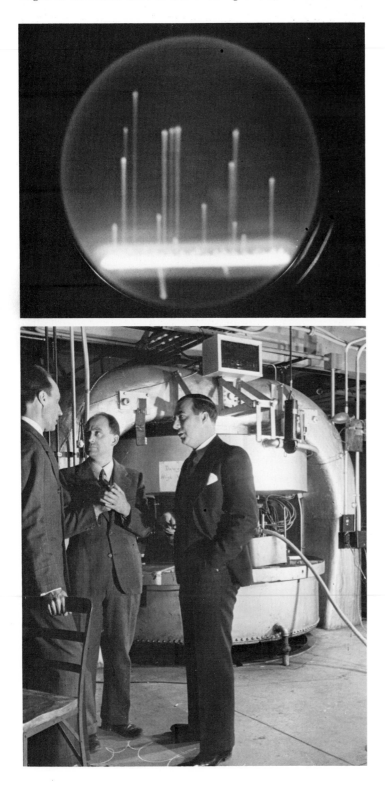

Enrico Fermi (left) is flanked by two Manhattan Project colleagues next to the Columbia University cyclotron, a device able to split atoms by neutron bombardment. The vertical pulses on a voltage indicator (above) record the bursts of energy released when U-235 atoms are split.

ide. The program began to gather momentum in the summer of 1940 when it became the responsibility of a newly formed National Defense Research Committee, an organization conceived by Roosevelt to assemble the best of the country's scientific talent. The chairman of the NDRC, Vannevar Bush, was President of the Carnegie Institution and a prominent scientific administrator.

Under Bush, the nuclear project received more money—$40,000 by September. Still, nothing of substance was accomplished until early in the summer of 1941; then the impetus for action came, with little warning, from an unexpected source.

Fugitive physicists had found haven in Britain as well as in the United States. Driven by wartime urgency and a shared fear of the Germans, they worked intensely on the possibility of developing an atomic bomb. In June of 1941 the British government sent Bush a top-secret report entitled "The Use of Uranium for a Bomb." Prepared by a committee code-named Maud, the report was based on work done in England by Otto Frisch, the man who while living in Denmark had first confirmed the German experiments and confided the secret to Niels Bohr. The Maud report confidently claimed that a bomb could be built within two years and that its effects would be cataclysmic. The report carefully detailed a method for separating U-235 from U-238, discussed plutonium as an explosive, proposed methods of detonating such a weapon and calculated that it could be made compact enough to be carried by air.

Bush took the report to Roosevelt and somberly advised him that one thing was certain: "If such an explosive were made it would be thousands of times more powerful than existing explosives, and its use might be determining." It was Bush's way of asserting that an atomic bomb, if built, could decide the outcome of the War.

Roosevelt reacted with alarm. If a few scientists in war-ravaged England had made such remarkable progress, how far had the Germans, working with Hitler's full support, advanced in the same time? After a year and a half of inactivity, the American nuclear project now was elevated to the top rank of the nation's priorities.

By October 1941 the project had become a special section, designated S-1, of the newly organized Office of Scientific Research and Development (OSRD). Bush, having

turned over the Defense Research Committee to James B. Conant of Harvard, took command of the new unit. For the project, Bush had the backing of a prestigious policy committee that included Conant, Secretary of War Henry L. Stimson, Chief of Staff George Marshall and Vice President Henry Wallace. By November, $300,000 had been committed to research contracts with universities and industrial laboratories. A few weeks later, the United States was at war, and the project assumed an even greater urgency.

Within six months, the program began to bear results: In May of 1942, physicists offered Bush five potential methods of extracting fissionable material. Ultimately the program concentrated on three of the methods, two for separating U-235 from U-238 and a third for creating plutonium. The first, called the gaseous-diffusion process, was assigned to a group at Columbia University under the leadership of Harold Urey. A second group, led by Ernest O. Lawrence at the University of California, sought to isolate U-235 by a process called electromagnetic separation. At the University of Chicago, Arthur Holly Compton, with Fermi as his resident genius, proposed to make plutonium as the by-product of a controlled chain reaction in a uranium pile.

No one was certain which, if any, of the three methods would work. To find out, and to begin the manufacture of the fissionable material, the bomb builders now undertook an engineering and construction project of unprecedented proportions—in effect, as Teller warned, they had to turn

Albert Einstein, whose pioneering theory outlining the relationship between matter and energy was demonstrated most graphically by the atomic bomb, makes notes in his study at Princeton University in 1943. It was Einstein's letter to President Franklin D. Roosevelt in 1939, in which the famed physicist discussed the possibility of a nuclear weapon, that got the United States started on the Manhattan Project.

"the whole of the United States" into a nuclear factory. For help in this monumental task, they turned to the nation's greatest contractor, the U.S. Army Corps of Engineers, and in September one of the corps's best officers was selected to oversee the project.

Colonel Leslie R. Groves emphatically did not want the job. After 24 years of Army construction work, including the building of the Pentagon, Groves had been promised a combat command and that was what he wanted. But Groves's superior officer, Major General Brehon Somervell, refused to let him back out. "Do this job right," said Somervell, "and it can win the War." As an added inducement, Groves was offered the star of a brigadier general.

A career officer, fourth in the West Point class of 1918, Groves knew when he was outgunned. And he was the ideal choice for the nearly impossible task at hand. The son of an Army chaplain, Groves was governed by a powerful sense of duty. Physically massive, by temperament curt, uncompromising and frequently tyrannical, he lived by one straightforward rule: Do it and see that it is done right.

At the time of his appointment, Groves's income, including a brigadier general's pay and allowances, was $663.40 a month. Before long, he was spending millions of dollars every day. At one point he had, in his own name, an astronomical checking account of $37.5 million—ready cash to buy uranium anywhere he could find it. Such financing procedures were deliberately devious, intended to prevent anyone—including members of Congress—from learning too much about the supersecret project.

Along with its new director, the project acquired a name, the Manhattan Engineer District, an obscurity intended to deflect attention from its real purpose. With Groves at the helm, the project speeded up at once. On the day of his appointment he met with his aide, Lieut. Colonel Kenneth Nichols, to discuss priorities. The top priority was uranium.

Until recently, Nichols told Groves, nobody—except the worried refugee scientists—had given much thought to stockpiling uranium. Nichols himself had undertaken a survey and found the metal unexpectedly scarce. Just 10 days earlier, however, an Assistant Secretary of State named Thomas Finletter had mentioned to him offhandedly that an acquaintance in New York City named Edgar Sengier apparently had a quantity of uranium. Finletter had been aware of the uranium stockpile for some time, but since the State Department knew nothing about the Manhattan Project, he had thought little about it. With Groves's approval, Nichols hurried to New York to see Sengier.

The man turned out to be a Belgian refugee who had fled the Nazis in 1939. He was President of the Union Minière du Haut-Katanga, the firm that owned and operated Shinkolobwe, the world's richest uranium mine in the Belgian Congo. He did have uranium, a lot of it.

Shortly before the outbreak of war, Sengier had been warned by a British scientist that uranium might someday be useful as a weapon. He never forgot that warning and in 1940, with Belgium overrun, he began to worry about a German invasion of the Congo. Late in the year he sent secret orders to Shinkolobwe to ship all available uranium ore direct to the United States by whatever means possible. As a result, 1,250 tons of high-grade uranium ore had been shipped from the Congo through the nearest open port, in Portuguese Angola, and was stored in 2,000 steel drums in a warehouse on Staten Island.

Sengier was blunt. "Now, are you here to talk or to do business?" he asked Nichols. Within an hour the American colonel left the Belgian émigré's office clutching a sheet of yellow scratch paper on which were scribbled the terms of the sale—$1.60 a pound, the lowest market price, four million dollars for the lot—and an agreement to sell any other ore that could be brought out of the Congo.

"I want to start hauling that uranium away tomorrow," Nichols told Sengier upon leaving.

"Quite all right with me," Sengier said. "Our lawyers can work out the contract later."

Securing a supply of uranium was only the first challenge the Manhattan Project had to overcome. From the outset the project was plagued by shortages, one of which came

A supervisor checks stacks of pure silver, part of the 14,000 tons of the precious metal borrowed from the U.S. Treasury for use as coils in the giant magnets required by the Manhattan Project's reactors.

This oval-shaped "race track" at the Clinton Engineer Works near Oak Ridge, Tennessee, part of an electromagnetic-separation plant for the production of uranium 235, is ribbed with magnets, each made by winding conductive silver wire around an iron core.

to light at Berkeley in the planning stage for Lawrence's electromagnetic-separation process. To construct his system on the grand scale required, Lawrence calculated he would need the world's largest magnets—each 250 feet long, and 100 times more powerful than the magnet in his laboratory cyclotron at the university. It would take thousands of miles of copper wire to wind the coils of these mammoth magnets. But war-industry demand for copper had all but exhausted the American supply; there was no longer enough copper in the country to complete machines of the size Lawrence needed. He wrestled with the problem, and came up with an extraordinary suggestion. "Why not use silver?" he asked Colonel Nichols. "It is an excellent conductor of electricity."

Nichols called on Undersecretary of the Treasury Daniel Bell and advised him that a government agency designated the Manhattan Engineer District needed a lot of silver.

"What for?" Bell naturally asked.

"It's top secret, Mr. Secretary," Nichols said. "All I can reveal is that it's for an important war project directed by the Army Engineers."

"How much silver?" Bell asked.

"Six thousand tons," Nichols replied.

"Young man," Bell replied reprovingly, "you may think of silver in tons, but the U.S. Treasury will always think of silver in troy ounces."

Bell admitted that the Treasury had troy ounces of silver on hand amounting to 47,000 tons, and another 39,000 tons formally reserved as backing for U.S. silver certificates. Lending silver would require the approval of Secretary of the Treasury Henry Morgenthau. This was obtained and eventually the Manhattan Project borrowed 14,000 tons of the precious metal, valued at $300 million, promising to return it all within six months after the War ended. A fleet of unmarked trucks picked up the silver bars at the West Point Depository in New York and hauled them to a plant in Car-

teret, New Jersey, where they were cast into cylinders. Then the silver was shipped to the Phelps Dodge Copper Products plant in Elizabeth, New Jersey, where it was extruded into narrow strips and rolled into doughnut-shaped bundles. The bundles were shipped to the Allis-Chalmers metals plant in Milwaukee, where the strips were insulated, then wound around giant steel cores to make Lawrence's magnets. (When the War was over, the Treasury got back all but 4.9 tons—or .035 of 1 per cent—of its silver.)

A similar shortage confronted Urey and his colleagues at Columbia, where they proposed to separate fissionable U-235 from U-238 in the form of uranium hexafluoride, a gas so fiercely corrosive that almost no material known to man could withstand it. The lone exception was pure nickel.

The scientists calculated that, in order to produce measurable quantities of U-235, their gaseous-diffusion plant would have to be built on a gigantic scale. They would need more than three million feet of piping in a range of sizes from six inches in diameter downward. It seemed likely the pipes would have to be manufactured from solid nickel, rather than nickel-plated steel. Nickel resists uniform plating, and even microscopic flaws in the plating would permit the gas to eat through the base material of the pipe. The smallest leak would jeopardize the entire process.

Groves consulted industry experts and came away with dismaying news. The nickel required by the Manhattan Engineer District was twice the U.S. annual production. And nickel was critical for other vital war industries, which needed the metal for such processes as hardening steel.

As he mulled over this latest problem, Groves remembered something that might be useful. Ten years earlier, while in charge of an antiaircraft searchlight procurement program, he had experienced trouble with the glass mirror in the searchlight then in use. Groves had sought help from a Swiss-born electroplating specialist named Blasius Bart at a small, family-run plant in Belleville, New Jersey. In time, Bart succeeded in plating a curved metal mirror for the lights. If anybody in America could satisfactorily nickel-plate the curved interior of steel pipes, Groves thought, Bart was the man.

It turned out that Blasius Bart had retired, but his 29-year-old son, Sieg, was now running the family plant. The younger Bart agreed to try to plate the pipe. It was slow work; experimenting with different methods and plating solutions, he met with failure after failure. Then he had an inspiration. Instead of submerging a 20-foot section of pipe in a tank of nickel-plating solution, why not use the pipe itself as the tank and pump the solution through it? For good measure, he tried rotating the pipe during the process, hoping to get a more uniform coating of nickel. It worked, and before long Sieg Bart had 400 workers plating miles of pipe. His invention reduced the amount of nickel required by 98 per cent.

While scientists and technologists grappled with the myriad problems that barred the way to production of fissionable material, General Groves and his lieutenants acquired land

A billboard at the Manhattan Project's Oak Ridge facility admonishes workers to maintain absolute silence during their off-duty hours concerning the top-secret project.

An oil painting depicts history's first man-made nuclear chain reaction at the University of Chicago on December 2, 1942. As Manhattan Project scientists observe the atomic pile from a balcony, Enrico Fermi, in light suit near the rail, makes calculations on his slide rule to determine when the pile will go critical.

for the prospective manufacturing plants. They sought isolated sites for two reasons: to hide the project from prying eyes, and to avert a mass tragedy should the inherently dangerous material somehow explode.

In September 1942, shortly after his appointment, Groves made his first real-estate purchase for the Manhattan Project: 54,000 acres of rolling Tennessee countryside about 18 miles from Knoxville, between the Great Smoky and the Cumberland Mountains. The Clinton Engineer Works near the town of Oak Ridge eventually housed the huge magnets and vacuum chambers of the electromagnetic process, the forest of pipes, pumps and valves of the gas-diffusion works, smaller thermal-diffusion and plutonium plants, and one of the world's largest electrical generating plants.

Oak Ridge was merely the first of four mammoth real-estate transactions Groves undertook. His second acquisition was a section of Illinois forest land about 20 miles west of Chicago. In the autumn of 1942, Compton and Fermi at the University of Chicago were on the verge of constructing the world's first atomic pile. Since nobody was certain that a chain reaction could be controlled, it was considered prudent to make the attempt somewhere distant from the university campus on Chicago's crowded South Side.

Prudence went by the board in early November, however, when a labor-union dispute held up construction of a reactor building at the forest site. Compton, armed with Fermi's confident prediction that the process was safe, now argued for building the pile in the cold and drafty squash courts under the west stands of the university's unused football stadium, Stagg Field. Rather unwillingly, but driven by haste, Groves agreed.

Building the Chicago pile turned out to be the dirtiest job the Manhattan Project undertook. Fermi himself laid the cornerstone on November 7, 1942, picking up a brick of purified graphite that measured 4⅛ by 4⅛ by 16½ inches and putting it down in one corner of the canvas-covered floor beneath Stagg Field. When he returned for a second brick, his hands were black.

Fermi's bricks were the first of 40,000 laid out in a circular space 24 feet in diameter. The bricks in alternate tiers were bored with holes spaced 8¼ inches apart to receive six-pound lumps of uranium or uranium oxide. The graphite arrived from Union Carbide in long rough bars that had to be sawed to size, planed smooth, and bored with the uranium holes. This finishing work added measurably to the graphite dust that clung like a Stygian ooze to every surface and soon made the floor as slippery as a skating rink.

Two crews, made up of mechanics and technicians aided occasionally by university students and the impatient scientists, took turns laying brick 24 hours a day. "If people knew what we were doing with a million and a half of their dollars they'd think we were crazy," remarked a scientist as he scrubbed away the grime at the end of a shift. The scrubbing was largely futile; half an hour after the bricklayers washed, graphite dust began to seep from their pores.

Tier by tier the black pile grew, while Fermi prowled around it making calculations on a six-inch slide rule. On December 1, when the column was more than 40 bricks high, the pile began to show signs of having a life of its own. Neutron counters on an instrument panel mounted on a balcony next to the pile began to click, and then click faster as each new tier of uranium-laden bricks was added.

Fermi ordered his assistants to insert cadmium-plated control rods, which were designed to trap neutrons and thus slow down the reaction. There were three such rods; one was manipulated mechanically from the control panel, another could be inserted or withdrawn by hand on Fermi's orders. The third rod, called the zip, was an emergency brake that would plunge rapidly into the pile from above if the chain reaction began to go wild.

By 4 p.m. the pile was 48 tiers high. Fermi took a last look around, pocketed his slide rule, and told his crew chief to add three more tiers to the pile. Then he coolly quit for the day, telling an assistant to be sure to lock in the control rods.

The next morning, with Compton and a score of associates in attendance, Fermi coaxed his atomic pile to life. At 9:45 a.m. he ordered the mechanically operated control withdrawn. Then the emergency zip was hauled up out of the pile and left dangling, fixed by rope and pulleys to a balancing weight. One of the staff stood by with an ax, prepared to chop the rope and let the zip drop back inside if anything went awry. As a further precaution, a three-man "suicide squad" stood on a platform above the pile with buckets of neutron-absorbing liquid cadmium to douse the pile if it threatened to run away.

Another aide stood beside the pile clutching the manual control rod, now presumably the last barrier to a chain reaction. "Pull it to thirteen feet," Fermi ordered at 10:37 a.m. The rod moved out, the neutron counters began to chatter and the pen of a recording device began to trace an upward moving line. The pile was indeed alive, although Fermi had not yet unleashed a self-sustained chain reaction.

Fermi worked his slide rule. "The trace will go to this point and level off," he said calmly. No one else in the room was nearly as composed. What if the reaction did not subside—would anyone there survive?

But the trace pen leveled at the point Fermi had predicted, and the counters quieted down. Fermi ordered the rod pulled out a little more and activity speeded up until, as he had forecast, it quieted again.

At noon, Fermi delivered a showman's *coup de théâtre.* "I'm hungry," he announced. "Let's go to lunch." He then led the way to the student cafeteria.

Returning to the pile that afternoon, Fermi, slide rule in hand, directed that the rod come out another foot. The clicking of the counters crescendoed to a sustained rattle, and the trace pen moved up and kept moving up without the previous leveling off. Fermi turned to Compton, smiling, and said, "The reaction is self-sustaining." It was 3:25 p.m., December 2, 1942.

Fermi let the chain reaction continue for 28 minutes; then, satisfied with the day's work, he ordered, "Zip in," and the world's first atomic pile obediently went dormant.

Compton returned to his office to call James Conant at Harvard. In an oblique salute to Fermi, the refugee from Fascist Italy, Compton said, "Jim, you'll be interested to know that the Italian navigator has landed in the New World."

"Were the natives friendly?" Conant asked. He was assured that they were. Although Fermi's functional atomic pile had not proved absolutely that such a machine could be used to manufacture fissionable plutonium, the scientists in Chicago were now confident that it could be done.

Nobody yet knew—within a factor of 10 to 1,000—how much plutonium or U-235 would be needed to build an explodable bomb. But in the wake of Fermi's success, scientists predicted that six reactors would be required to produce plutonium on a usable scale. Each of them would have to be many times larger than the 500-ton midget hidden under the football stands at the University of Chicago.

The question of where to put the huge plutonium-making reactors loomed large on Groves's list of problems. An early suggestion to locate them at Oak Ridge had to be abandoned. Since atomic piles were potentially dangerous, the designers wanted to give them plenty of elbowroom. Oak Ridge, already designated as the site of the production plants for U-235, simply did not have enough space to provide a margin of safety.

On New Year's Eve, 1942, a land-survey team headed by a hydraulic engineer, Lieut. Colonel Franklin Matthias, returned to Groves's office in Washington with the answer. Near the straggling village of Hanford, Washington, they had found half a million acres that seemed ideal. The tract lay on the Columbia River, which would provide the water needed to cool the reactors, and was within easy reach of ample power from the new Grand Coulee and Bonneville Dams. Moreover, the region was arid sagebrush country; its sparse population consisted mostly of the operators of a few

At a change of shifts, workers pour out of the front gate at the Oak Ridge facility, which produced fissionable uranium and plutonium for atomic bombs. The sign at right lists winners of a work-incentive contest.

irrigated cherry and apricot orchards. Groves inspected the land on January 16 and approved, stopping for a snack of crackers at Hanford's small general store. Condemnation proceedings began on February 8.

Hanford was not the only large tract that Groves acquired for the Manhattan Project that winter. On December 7, 1942, he had signed condemnation papers for a boys' boarding school and adjacent land on a remote mountain plateau in the New Mexico desert. At Los Alamos, as the place was called, the far-flung endeavors of the Manhattan Project were supposed to merge and produce a final product. In the spring of 1943, a team of scientists under the direction of J. Robert Oppenheimer, a brilliant 39-year-old physicist, gathered there to commence the most secretive, dangerous and eventful engineering project ever undertaken by the U.S. government: the design and construction of the atomic bomb. Their work could progress only so far without the fissionable material that would make up the heart of the bomb, but the effort to produce a supply of plutonium and U-235 was now proceeding at full tilt.

By mid-1943 more than 30 American industrial firms—companies preeminent in chemicals, construction, engineering, metal processing and electrical equipment—were deeply engaged in work for the Manhattan Project. Many of them had signed on with reluctance, only after earnest assurances that the work required was absolutely vital to the war effort. The hesitation of company presidents and boards of directors was understandable. Most were already laboring under a heavy load of high-priority war contracts. Many of the tasks they were asked to perform for the Manhattan Project were untried. In some cases, new tools and methods had to be invented before the work could even begin. And the manpower diverted from other important assignments was staggering: At its peak, the Manhattan Project commanded the energies of more than 600,000 Americans.

Another good reason why companies were reluctant to join the project was the irritating mantle of secrecy that General Groves imposed. Groves was a near-fanatic about security. So far as he was able, he saw to it that no individual in private industry—except for a handful of key executives—ever learned more than the minimum needed to do his or her job. Consequently, the legions of workers labored in total ignorance of the purpose of their work. Women hired to process material for filters for the gaseous-diffusion process, for example, were never told why they were shifted to another project during menstruation. The unstated reason was concern that the women's hands, which might perspire more than normally at that time, would deposit organic

27

matter on the delicate material, despite the white gloves they wore at work.

Groves did not exempt himself from the regimen of obsessive security. To render himself as inconspicuous as possible, he often wore civilian clothes on the job. When traveling in public conveyances with classified documents, he customarily sat on them. And he packed a .32-caliber pistol in his belt to protect the enormous secrets in both his briefcase and his head.

Groves's insistence on security was only one of the reasons he clashed repeatedly with the aloof, independent and temperamental civilian scientists. From the first, the physicists resented being subjected to military control. They disliked the speed with which Groves pushed the program, and, in any case, they considered themselves far better qualified to build a bomb than any collection of Army officers and industrial engineers.

The simmering friction threatened to boil over at Los Alamos. To begin with, life in the New Mexico wasteland was lonely and primitive. And in the opinion of the science and ordnance group stationed there under Oppenheimer, Groves made it unnecessarily worse.

If security was tight elsewhere in the Manhattan Project, it became a strait jacket at Los Alamos. Groves imposed mail censorship and forbade travel farther than Albuquerque, 100 miles away. He discouraged communication between the scientists at Los Alamos and their colleagues and friends at other Manhattan Project installations and in universities around the country. He established perimeter guards who operated under strict orders. When Commander William S. Parsons, a Navy ordnance officer, appeared at the gate wearing summer khakis, he was refused admittance because the Army sentry failed to recognize his uniform. The sentry telephoned his sergeant to report: "We've caught a spy. A guy down here is trying to get in and his uniform is as phony as a three-dollar bill."

When the scientists at Los Alamos continued to exhibit a strong sense of independence, Groves decided to bring them to heel in a drastic way—by inducting them into the Army and putting them into uniform. "All I asked of the civilian scientists in the Army," he later observed in aggrieved tones, "was that they be able to wear the uniform, they be able to salute, and they be able to stand at attention and say,

'Yes, sir' when an officer spoke to them." Such concessions Groves never got. His induction scheme spurred an open rebellion among the scientists, and he was forced to back down on pain of losing his entire crew.

Groves retreated without grace. He continued to regard the scientists as disobedient children and at times referred to them as "crackpots." But in the uneasy truce that prevailed, the contending parties proceeded with their work.

At Hanford, Oak Ridge and Los Alamos, the gigantic plants grew apace. Instant towns, complete with schools and churches, were erected to accommodate the thousands upon thousands of workers. Recruiting teams roamed the country, signing up new employees.

At all three sites, technologists wrestled with a succession of problems, solving each with brilliance and ingenuity. One of the most baffling concerned the pumps to be employed in the miles-long cascades of pipe for the gaseous-diffusion process at Oak Ridge. The demand made upon these thousands of pumps went far beyond anything in engineering experience. The pumps would have to drive the corrosive uranium hexafluoride at high speeds. They had to be totally leakproof and they had to operate continuously without any lubrication because the uranium hexafluoride would explode on contact with grease or oil.

After months of failure and frustration, a near-perfect pump was finally designed by George Watts, chief engineer for Standard Oil of Indiana, and Judson Swearingen, a young chemical engineer from Texas.

For more than two years, another apparently impossible task dogged the scientists working on the gaseous-diffusion process. The challenge was to develop a material from which to fashion thousands of filters that would separate U-235 from the heavier U-238. The filters had to be corrosion-proof, dependably uniform in quality, and porous—with millions of infinitesimal holes in every square inch. The search for the right material proved so traumatically demanding that Harold Urey, the project leader, had to be shifted to less exhausting responsibilities.

It had been a fairly simple matter to choose the basic filter material, powdered nickel, which was corrosion-proof. But the subsequent problems of uniformity, porosity, strength enough to prevent crumbling, and the capacity to be weld-

In a remote valley near Hanford, Washington, a factory complex for the production of fissionable plutonium sprawls along a bank of the Columbia River. A labor force of 45,000 completed the facility in one year.

ed proved all but insurmountable. Dozens of chemists, experimenting independently, turned out different samples of about postcard size. Some were fairly good, others so fragile that they were dismissed contemptuously as "lace curtains." Then, on the night of June 19, 1943, working late in his laboratory in Jersey City, New Jersey, a research chemist named Clarence Johnson produced a sample that met every demanding test.

That was, however, only the beginning of an answer. Instead of a laboratory sample, the process would require one million square feet of material. Mass production promised endless problems, not the least of which was the design of furnaces used to fuse the nickel powder. But by the spring of 1944 a suitable furnace had been designed and built by an engineer in Salem, Ohio, named Sam Keener, an eccentric former cowboy with a sixth-grade education whose preferred office attire featured cowboy boots, silver spurs and embroidered rodeo shirts.

At Hanford, Washington, the intense radioactivity in the reactors designed to separate the plutonium from irradiated uranium forced plant personnel to maintain a safe distance. To run the plants largely by remote control, whole families of mechanical manipulators had to be invented. And to oversee the manipulators at work and inspect the seething

furnaces of the reactors, new optical systems had to be devised. A serious hitch developed when it was discovered that radiation turned glass lenses black and useless. That problem was solved when researchers learned that certain clear plastics were immune to the blackening effect; thereafter the lenses of periscopes and other optical instruments used near uranium were made of plastic.

In November of 1943, the immense and complicated labors at Oak Ridge, Tennessee, were about to bear first fruit. The alpha, or first, unit of Lawrence's electromagnetic separation plant was ready to be turned on. The heart of this process was the magnets wound with borrowed U.S. Treasury silver; they were the largest ever built, each weighing from 3,000 to 10,000 tons and each containing 12 to 21 tons of silver in its coil. Their powerful pull would snatch hammers and other tools out of the hands of unwary workers, inflicting bruises and skinned knuckles if the workers failed to let go in time. No woman employee's hairdo was safe—if she ventured too near a magnet, the hairpins would fly out of her coiffure and glue themselves immovably to the magnet case. A more serious by-product of the magnets' immense power became evident later when 14-ton steel tanks were pulled as much as three inches out of position, in the proc-

ess popping loose the plumbing lines connecting the tanks.

A far more severe setback occurred when the alpha unit was activated. Soon after power was fed into the monster magnets, they began to short-circuit and cut out. When no other diagnostic measure solved the problem, General Groves ordered the steel casing of one magnet cut open to see if anything inside was amiss. Plenty was. Somehow, particles of rust and other metallic debris had found their way into the circulating oil used to cool the great machine. Groves was furious, at first suspecting sabotage, then blaming sloppy workmanship. The magnets had to be shipped back to Allis-Chalmers in Wisconsin to be cleaned and rewound, while the program at Oak Ridge was put on hold.

The first of the three reactors under construction at Hanford was ready to be fired up in early September, 1944. Before the uranium was loaded in, Groves telephoned from Washington, D.C., to Franklin Matthias, his chief engineer on the scene: ''Colonel, I'll advise you of one thing. You'd better be there when they start running that plant. If it blows up, you just jump right in the middle of it—it will save you a heck of a lot of trouble.''

The reactor, designated Pile B, did not blow up. But after a deceptively smooth start it began to behave in a mystifying manner. As he had been in Chicago, Enrico Fermi was there with his slide rule to supervise the loading of the immense pile. Unlike the Chicago reactor, in which the uranium slugs were embedded directly in graphite bricks, Pile B was to be loaded by sliding hundreds of long rods of uranium encased in aluminum into holes already cut through the graphite and outer shielding.

Loading started on September 13. In two days the pile began to generate some heat, and Fermi ordered the control rods inserted. So far everything was going well. Fermi carefully built up the power until September 27. With everything still in apparent good order, he decided to step up the reaction. The chilly waters of the Columbia River were circulating through the pile's veins and the control rods were raised just after midnight. By 2 o'clock in the morning, still far below its peak, the pile was generating more power than any previous chain reaction.

Then at 3 a.m., Pile B unaccountably lost power. By 6:30 a.m. it was cold and seemed completely lifeless. The baffled scientists puzzled over the possible causes: sabotage, leaks somewhere, contaminated water from the river? Nothing explained for certain how the pile could possibly have expired, but it had; Pile B looked very much like a $300-million cadaver.

The next day, while the frustrated operators were still hunting desperately for a clue, the pile resurrected itself as mysteriously as it had died. With no apparent help from anybody, it came alive and was soon producing 9,000 kilowatts, the level it had reached the day before. Then, just as abruptly, it dwindled, went cold again and died.

Among the troubleshooters called in to diagnose Pile B's ailment was John Wheeler, the Princeton physicist who had been Niels Bohr's junior associate. Wheeler studied graphs of Pile B's performance and wondered whether some short-lived fission product might be poisoning the reactor, or causing it to poison itself. He took his theory to Fermi and they set to work looking for some radioactive gas that the pile might be generating whose rate of decay—or half

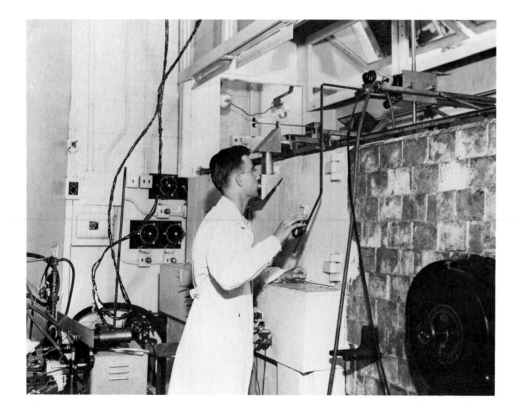

Protected by a wall of lead and brick six inches thick, a University of Chicago scientist manipulates lethal radioactive material by remote control. Overhead mirrors and a periscope enable him to see what he is doing.

life—would fit the intervals between the reactor's demise and revival. They found it, a gas called xenon 135 whose half life was 9.4 hours. Fermi went to work with his slide rule and decided that the xenon poisoning could be cured by increasing the reactor's uranium load 25 per cent. This was done, and Pile B gave no more trouble. On Christmas Day it yielded its first irradiated uranium slugs. The slugs were sent to separation plants where, in January of 1945, remote-control devices recovered from them the newly created plutonium.

The success at Hanford drew cheers from Los Alamos. Condemned by necessity to theory and guesswork, Robert Oppenheimer and his bomb designers had grown increasingly desperate to get their hands on some genuine fissionable material. When Hanford at last produced its first bit of plutonium, Colonel Matthias decided to escort the precious metal at least part of the way to New Mexico in person.

The plutonium was packed in a heavy stainless-steel container suspended inside a rectangular wooden box about two feet high. Matthias put the box in his automobile and drove to Portland, Oregon, where he took a train for Los Angeles. There he was met by an Army officer who had not been told what he would be carrying.

"You have a bedroom on the train back to Los Alamos, I hope?" Matthias asked. The courier said the trains were so crowded all he had been able to get was an upper berth.

"Do you realize that what you're going to carry is pretty valuable?" Matthias demanded.

"What do you mean 'valuable,' sir?" the officer asked.

"I mean that it cost three hundred million dollars to make it!" The electrified officer wangled a bedroom and reached Los Alamos safely with his package on February 2, 1945.

Oak Ridge took a little longer to begin producing measurable quantities of U-235. Not until March 1945 did the transport of U-235 to Los Alamos begin. Then, once each week, heavily armed guards in an unmarked car drove out of the Oak Ridge gates and headed for Knoxville, where they boarded the 12:50 p.m. train for Chicago and locked themselves in a reserved compartment. In Chicago they turned over their special suitcases packed with nickel containers of U-235 to guards who carried it west on the Santa Fe *Chief.* The next day the cargo was delivered to a desert way station near Los Alamos.

Considering how little they had to work with, Oppenheimer's bomb designers in New Mexico had made remarkable progress. As early as April 1943 they concluded that U-235 could be exploded by fixing a piece of it to the muzzle of a gun and firing another chunk into it from the breech, creating what they termed a "critical mass." They also discussed another possible detonation method called implosion. This called for surrounding a hollow sphere of fissionable material with explosive charges that—set off within millionths of a second—would compress the sphere into a critical mass. But there were a host of questions they could not answer, including how many ounces, pounds, kilograms or tons of U-235 or plutonium it would take to achieve that critical mass. When they did find out, in the middle of 1945, the magic figures turned out to be about 15 kilograms of U-235, or about five kilograms of plutonium.

The processes of determining these vital weights proved extraordinarily dangerous. One method involved a jury-rigged contraption that the scientists aptly called the guillotine. To operate it, they dropped a small piece of fissionable material through a hole in a larger piece. If at the moment of proximity the total mass was at or near criticality, a brief chain reaction was generated. Only half-facetiously, the scientists called the process "tickling the dragon's tail." One of the experimenters, a Canadian named Louis Slotin, was killed during a similar experiment when he suffered a lethal dose of radiation. Slotin's death was one of eight fatal accidents reported by General Groves during the Manhattan Project. Five other staff members were electrocuted, one was gassed and one died in a fall.

When it became clear that the production rate of U-235

Researchers at Los Alamos brought this pile of radioactive uranium slugs almost to a critical mass by dropping a smaller uranium slug through the pile's center. Such experiments, designed to determine the amount of uranium needed for a bomb, were so dangerous that the scientists nervously referred to them as "tickling the dragon's tail."

would permit the building of only one uranium bomb, the experimenters at Los Alamos turned their attention to the delicate problems of making a bomb from plutonium. Only one third as much plutonium was required to produce a critical mass, but one of the many baffling peculiarities of the man-made element was that it resisted being set off by the gun detonator. Soon 600 men were working instead to produce a reliable trigger for plutonium using the implosion technique. Eventually they succeeded, and the product of their combined efforts emerged as "Fat Man," the first atomic bomb ever built. But a monumental question remained: Would it work?

There was one way to find out, and a proper place was sought to test Fat Man. The site had to be flat, remote, far removed from prying eyes. Good weather, or the prospect of it, seemed a necessity. And the place had to be uninhabited. Groves insisted on that. He had no desire to tangle with Harold L. Ickes, the powerful and terrible-tempered Secretary of the Interior, if the test should by chance hurt or even discommode a single unwary citizen. Said Groves of Ickes: "His curiosity and insatiable desire to have his own way in every detail would have caused difficulties, and we already had too many."

The test site finally chosen—and code-named Trinity—lay in the heart of the Army Air Forces' Alamogordo Bombing Range, about 200 miles south of Los Alamos. It was a heat-seared, pitiless region known to the early Spanish explorers who crossed it as Jornada del Muerto (Journey of Death). The nearest points of habitation were the towns of Socorro and Carrizozo, more than 20 miles away. Amarillo, Texas, some 300 miles downwind, was the population center of greatest concern to Groves, should radioactive fallout require the evacuation of civilians.

On July 15, 1945, atop a 100-foot steel tower at Trinity, Fat Man lay waiting, sheltered under a sheet-steel roof, all of its intricate innards meticulously assembled around a hollow shell of plutonium. A five-man guard detail remained near the tower to ensure that Fat Man was not disturbed.

The bomb's other attendants were scattered among a command dugout and two other blastproof bunkers about five miles away, and at Trinity base camp 10 miles from the explosion point, designated Ground Zero. They included Groves, Oppenheimer, Bush, Conant, Fermi and most of the other leading physicists, as well as technicians assigned to trigger the event. This was the culmination of three years of stupefying effort and the expense of more than two billion dollars; tension rose to fever pitch. Watching Oppenheimer, upon whom the ultimate responsibility now rested, Groves found him pale, haggard with exhaustion and on the verge of collapse.

Fermi, by nervous contrast, was in a playful mood. He circulated among his distinguished colleagues offering to take wagers on whether Fat Man would set fire to the atmosphere and, if it did, whether it would wipe out merely New Mexico or the entire planet. At first Groves was irritated, finding Fermi's banter in bad taste. On further consideration he decided that the Italian was only trying to joke away everybody's stress, perhaps including his own.

After two agonizing delays caused by unpredicted rain, Groves and Oppenheimer agreed that the test should occur at 5:30 a.m. on July 16. Thirty minutes before that time, a seven-man arming crew finished the final checks on Fat Man, turned on a floodlight to illuminate its tower and retreated in jeeps. The bomb rested alone in the desert. At the command dugout the crew that would detonate the bomb using an electric cable went belowground where Oppenheimer, strained beyond endurance, clung to a post for support. At base camp the observers lay on their stomachs, facing away from Fat Man, and squeezed their eyes shut. The countdown began at 5:10, called off in intervals of minutes, then seconds. At 5:29 the counter shouted, "Zero!"

Many witnesses later struggled for words to describe what followed. William Laurence, *The New York Times* science reporter who was the Manhattan Project's chronicler, came close: "On that moment hung eternity," he wrote. "Time stood still. Space contracted to a pin point. It was as though the earth had opened and the skies split. One felt as though he had been privileged to witness the birth of the world."

Perhaps it was Oppenheimer who summoned the most prescient words. As the bomb's fireball ascended into man-made daylight over the desert, the stunned scientist thought of an ominous line from the Bhagavad-Gita, a sacred Hindu text: "I am become Death, the shatterer of worlds."

In the predawn darkness of July 16, 1945, an incandescent fireball from the first atomic explosion boils skyward over the Army Air Forces' Alamogordo Bombing Range in the New Mexico desert.

COUNTDOWN IN THE DESERT

shallow crater surrounded by scorched earth marks the New Mexico desert at Ground Zero after the detonation of the first atomic bomb on July 16, 1945.

A SECRETIVE SETTING FOR GENIUS AT WORK

The sheer brain power gathered at a former boys' school on a remote mesa 35 miles northwest of Santa Fe, New Mexico, was arguably the greatest such concentration in history. Certainly it was the most secret. The mysterious base that replaced the Los Alamos Ranch School in February of 1943 swelled eventually to some 6,000 inhabitants, yet so tightly guarded was its mission that even after two years of close proximity, people in Santa Fe still wondered only half in jest whether it manufactured windshield wipers for submarines, or perhaps put together the front ends of horses for the cavalry. In fact, the unparalleled assemblage of intellect on the "Hill" was focused feverishly upon the creation of the atomic bomb.

Los Alamos was chosen as the Manhattan Project's central laboratory because it was isolated from most distractions, was surrounded by government-owned land, and was far enough from either coast to be safe from enemy attack. The site also had an influential backer—J. Robert Oppenheimer, the laboratory's scientific chief, who owned a small ranch nearby and contended that the majestic natural surroundings would advance the vital work at hand.

Oppenheimer also insisted that families be permitted to join the scientists at Los Alamos—a concession that almost choked Brigadier General Leslie R. Groves, the determined manager of the project. Groves dreaded becoming bogged down in the "fuss and feathers" of family life. For their part, the families came to detest Groves as the enforcer of a military regimen that included censorship, the use of aliases and the unsmiling challenges of armed guards.

Still, for both scientists and their families (who were kept as ignorant of the work as the rest of the world) there was always the compensation that Oppenheimer had promised: the breathtaking scenery, the mountains and canyons just beyond the barbed wire. And for the scientists there was the excitement of working alongside such brilliant thinkers as Niels Bohr, Enrico Fermi and Edward Teller. As one newly minted physicist attached to the project later recalled: "These were very great men indeed."

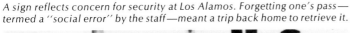

A sign reflects concern for security at Los Alamos. Forgetting one's pass—termed a "social error" by the staff—meant a trip back home to retrieve it.

Project chief Leslie Groves (left) works with the man he chose to lead "the greatest collection of eggheads ever"—physicist J. Robert Oppenheimer.

In their scoutlike uniforms, students attend graduation exercises at the Los Alamos Ranch School. The Indians, from nearby pueblos, danced during the ceremony and sold crafts.

COMMANDEERING A REMOTE CAMPUS

During the summer of 1942, the Los Alamos Ranch School began to receive baffling military attention. Low-flying planes buzzed the campus. Uniformed men appeared on the grounds, looking around appraisingly, talking to no one. On December 7—one year after Pearl Harbor—the school learned why: The U.S. Army wanted the site for a top-secret project.

School authorities were given just two months to close down. Classes were accelerated so seniors could graduate; during final exams, the first bulldozers arrived.

Some 3,000 construction workers and engineers quickly transformed the picturesque little academy into a dust-plagued boom town. Houses, laboratories and support buildings went up along with power lines to serve them. And where 10 years earlier there had been no road at all, a paved highway soon was alive with traffic in scientists, equipment and supplies.

Workmen widen, level and pave the original road from Santa Fe to Los Alamos in late 1943. The last l

was so steep and tortuous that travelers sometimes feared their cars would slide off one of the sharp, gravel switchbacks and tumble to the canyon floor.

Mounted guards patrol the rugged edge of the mesa. One scientist, annoyed by the strict security, found a hole in the fence and teased the guards at a nearby gate by checking out, returning unseen through the hole, then exiting again moments later.

The flat-roofed houses of McKeeville—named for the company that built them—line one of the dirt streets that turned to quagmires after rain and kicked u

A BOOM TOWN RUN BY THE BOOK

Prefabs, trailers and Quonset huts soon dwarfed the Ranch School at Los Alamos, and the town kept growing. Its population, expected to peak at 100, passed 5,000 within a year. It was a young and vigorous group—the average adult age was 25. Not least of the town's explosions, as General Groves complained, was the baby boom.

Los Alamos had to be fed, housed and controlled—all according to the Army's book. Barbed wire circled the 54,000-acre site, guards were everywhere, and a scientist might have to prove his identity before he could enter his own house. Top administrators lived in old faculty log cabins, dubbed "Bathtub Row" because they had the only tubs in town. But home for most was a jerry-built duplex or drab hut on a street with no lights, pavement or name.

Civilians grew adept at softening the hard military edges. They organized an amateur theater and a symphony orchestra. They dragooned the Military Police to keep an eye on their children. They even got around food rationing until unbending WACs replaced the more relaxed Pueblo Indians as commissary employees. And when necessary, the civilians rebelled. On one occasion wives and children held a tea party around a favorite tree to keep a soldier from bulldozing it—in order, he said, that planting might begin.

choking clouds of dust during the long dry spells.

Residents shop at the Los Alamos commissary, where groceries were sold at 10 per cent above cost.

Soldiers and civilians relax at the post exchange, which offered a jukebox and a soda fountain.

41

A NUCLEAR LABORATORY BUILT FROM SCRATCH

The first scientists arrived at Los Alamos in April 1943 to find a finished movie theater and an empty laboratory. The construction workers had first built what they knew how to build. And they had no experience in nuclear physics.

So the scientists had to become architects, equipment procurers, even laborers—and they arranged things to satisfy themselves. It was not an easy task: "What we were trying to do," wrote one scientist, "was build a new laboratory in the wilds of New Mexico with nothing to start with except the library of Horatio Alger books that those boys in the Ranch School read, and the pack equipment they used going horseback riding, none of which helped us very much in getting neutron-producing accelerators."

Within three months, not one but four accelerators were in use—"some sort of record," boasted one scientist. The cluster of inelegant buildings that housed them at the center of Los Alamos was called Tech Area; it spread in all directions as the work increased. Every morning at 7:30 sharp a factory whistle called the town to its task. From then until evening, and often late into the night, an odd assortment of physicists, engineers and machinists struggled at the thousand aspects of their single job: to design and build the atomic bomb.

Laboratory buildings sprawl across the Tech Area at Los Alamos. Security officers roamed through the labs at night, checking for unlocked doors and safes.

The world's first reactor to use enriched uranium stands half completed in a Los Alamos lab. The reactor produced neutrons and gamma rays, which scientists used to study the effects of nuclear radiation on such materials as metals and plastics.

Three of Los Alamos' scientific leaders confer informally: from left, experimental physicists Ernest O. Lawrence and Enrico Fermi, and theoretical physicist I. I. Rabi. Color-coded badges admitted scientists to different labs; Lawrence wears a white one, which opened all doors.

Scientists pull a trolley of radioactive material from its storage shelter—a primitive method of avoiding radiation exposure.

Official vehicles wait their turn at a security checkpoint on the Trinity test site. The Military Police guards operated out of trucks and from temporary stations set up under tents.

THE DESOLATE TEST SITE NAMED TRINITY

To test the bomb, a site was needed that would at once satisfy science, safety and security. It had to be far enough from Los Alamos to seem unrelated, yet be within easy reach. It had to have flat topography and good weather to ensure reliable measurements. And it had to be isolated.

A search committee considered and rejected an empty valley in Colorado, sand bars off the Texas coast, and a California island before it chose a desolate 18-by-24-mile stretch of the Alamogordo Bombing Range, 200 miles south of Los Alamos, in a desert named Jornada del Muerto—Journey of Death. Oppenheimer called the site Trinity after a sonnet by John Donne, who begged the "three-personed God" to "break, blow, burn, and make me new."

By the summer of 1945, more than 200 scientists and soldiers had set up camp at Trinity to prepare for the test. Many more shuttled between Trinity and Los Alamos, inspecting the work, delivering supplies. Everybody arriving at Trinity was confined to the camp, with only endless work, local fare—including antelope steak—and scorpions to make life interesting.

Trinity base camp bakes in the desert basin. The isolated camp relied o

teamsters to deliver tons of scientific equipment and supplies and to make up for poor communications by ferrying messages back and forth to Los Alamos.

The workers above stack crates of TNT on a wooden tower, then have their picture taken (right) in May 1945. The men who built the platform out of railroad ties and lumber were not told about the test until it was over.

A DRESS REHEARSAL USING TNT

The test was intended to answer numerous questions about the bomb's power, blast patterns and fallout. But the equipment on which the test depended—much of it as new as the bomb itself—had to be tested first. Instruments had to be calibrated, cameras checked, procedures rehearsed. Authorities ordered a scaled-down pretest, and workmen stacked 100 tons of TNT 18 feet high atop a 25-foot tower.

Instruments were placed at scaled distances from the blast site. Tubes of radioactive matter were inserted amid the TNT to test levels of fallout. Then, before dawn on May 7, 1945, the TNT was set off. It lit up the desert sky with an eerie orange fireball that changed to a mushroom cloud and rose 15,000 feet—and would have been memorable, some said, had it not been so quickly eclipsed by the real thing.

Technicians fill tubes with fission by-products for distribution among TNT crates to produce radioactive fallout.

One hundred tons of exploding TNT generate a fireball that was visible 60 miles away at Alamogordo.

Jumbo (left) arrives at a railroad siding in Pope, New Mexico, after a roundabout journey—a continual search for adequate clearance—from the plant that built it in Barberton, Ohio. Below, tractors pull Jumbo to Trinity; the 30-mile trip took several days.

A 214-TON WHITE ELEPHANT

So much rare plutonium was to be risked in the New Mexico test that scientists in 1944 searched for a way to salvage it in case the high explosives that were to trigger the nuclear reaction did no more than crack the bomb's shell.

Various recovery schemes called for exploding the bomb in water, sand or earth.

In the event of a failed test, the plutonium could then be retrieved from the containing element. But that element would also corrupt the measurements that were the ultimate reason for the test.

The solution was Jumbo—a huge metal tank designed by Los Alamos engineers to stretch but not burst during the trigger explosion, while disintegrating in a successful nuclear blast. Jumbo weighed 214 tons, was 25 feet long and 12 feet wide, and had a steel hide 14 inches thick. It was shipped

from Ohio on a custom-made flatcar to a specially built railroad siding in Pope, New Mexico, then towed to Trinity atop a gigantic, 64-wheeled trailer.

But by May 1945, when Jumbo arrived, plutonium was no longer so scarce. The scientists had new faith in their trigger mechanism and new doubts about Jumbo's effect upon measurements. Thus the immense white elephant, which had cost $150,000 to build, was relegated to sideshow status in the atomic test.

Jumbo hangs upended from the steel tower where it endured the nuclear explosion, approximately 800 feet from Ground Zero, as a rough test of the blast's power.

Outside the McDonald ranch house, shown at top, technicians carefully unload plutonium from the sedan on whose back seat it rode from Los Alamos.

SETTING THE STAGE FOR "FAT MAN"

As the test date approached, the pace at Trinity grew as oppressive as the desert heat. Crews worked 18- and 24-hour days in 100° F. temperatures to lay thousands of miles of electrical cable and to pave new roads intended to smooth the way for deli-cate equipment. Seismographs and other recording devices were installed, phone and public-address systems hooked up. Vital supplies came daily; once, to ensure prompt delivery, 24 rolls of recording paper were rushed from Chicago in a private train compartment usually used by VIPs.

On July 11, 1945, an Army sedan delivered the plutonium from Los Alamos. An old ranch house at Trinity had been made into a sterile lab for assembly of the bomb's nuclear core, which was then driven to a tent under the 100-foot tower at Ground Zero. There, on July 13, technicians put 13.5 pounds of plutonium inside 2.5 tons of explosives to form Fat Man—the world's first atomic bomb. At 8 a.m. the next day, Fat Man was lifted to a metal shack on the tower. An hour later detonators were attached, and all was ready.

Flash bombs are positioned on posts to illuminate the predawn darkness, ensuring enough light for cameras to record the last moments before detonation.

Firmly in the clutch of enormous pincers, Fat Man is prepared for winching to the top of the tower at Ground Zero on the morning of July 14, 1945.

Fat Man, fully assembled, awaits the countdown in its steel shed atop the 100-foot Trinity tower, which has been wired with detonation and measurement cables.

A TENSE WAIT NEAR GROUND ZERO

Sunday, July 15, the day before the test, was devoted to checking equipment, praying and—as the official schedule put it—"looking for rabbit's feet and four-leaf clovers." No one at Trinity knew what to expect. Scientists offered bets on expected yields that ranged from 100 to 45,000 tons of TNT. A mock-heroic poem made light of the scientists' fears that, with "necks to Truman's ax uncurled," they were about to fire "the flop heard 'round the world."

Many there feared the bomb would succeed too well, destroying all of Trinity, or Alamogordo or New Mexico—even the world. Soldiers dressed in civilian clothing and traveled to towns as far as 100 miles from Ground Zero to record shock waves—and gather evidence in case damage suits were filed. Others roamed in jeeps and on horseback, ready to evacuate nearby villages and ranches.

Vehicles also stood ready to evacuate the scientists and observers who, early on July 16, gathered in the shockproof control centers located 10,000 yards north, west and south of Ground Zero. Some observers waited outside the bunkers, lying flat, their faces turned away from the blast. All had been issued protective glasses; some in the chill darkness applied Army-issue suntan lotion to their exposed skin. Back at Los Alamos, a few watched from balconies or climbed nearby mountains to see the test, nearly 200 miles away.

At 5:10 a.m. the countdown began. Oppenheimer gripped a post to keep from collapsing from fatigue and worn nerves. Just before 5:30, soldiers on patrol 30 miles away told a restaurant owner to step outside, promising he would "see something the world has never seen before." As the last second ticked off, the announcer at the south control center dropped his microphone and shouted "Zero!"

Banked with earth, a photographic bunker has three portholes facing the tower. Cameras were set at speeds up to 8,000 frames per second to capture the instant of detonation.

Concrete and earthen bunkers at the south control center face north, nearly six miles from Ground Zero. The bunkers housed the main firing and instrument panels, and an assemblage of very important persons.

"THE DAY THE SUN ROSE TWICE"

Then there was light, brighter than any before it, light that would have outshone the noonday sun and been visible on Venus or Mars. It began as a brilliant, bleaching white, then deepened to yellow, peach and purple as the roiling fireball spiraled upward, spewing flame and trailing a skirt of molten sand. It lent to everything a preternatural clarity and suffused all with a warmth derived from a core heat that was four times greater than that of the sun.

Among the observers, the response was awed silence. One scientist thought the air itself was on fire. Another, watching monitoring equipment, took the bomb for a dud until he noticed the light and realized that his needles had jumped off their scales. Men were knocked down when the shock wave hit seconds after the blast, and they were deafened by the roar that followed.

Then came relief, even unscientific elation: The observers on one hill broke into

.006 SECOND

.016 SECOND

.034 SECOND

2 SECONDS

4 SECONDS

6 SECONDS

a jig while others writhed in a snake dance through the south control center.

Agents in Albuquerque and Sante Fe saw the incredible light and wondered if anyone closer had survived. Hundreds of miles away, tremors were felt and windows rattled. Civilians thought an airborne bomber had exploded, or the Japanese had invaded, or a natural disaster had occurred—one variously suspected to be an earthquake, a meteor crash or an electrical storm. A woman on the Arizona border reported that the sun rose twice that day, once very quickly. Horses in stables whinnied hysterically, toads fell silent, dogs shivered all morning in the desert heat. A GI sleeping off a drunk at Trinity base camp leaped awake at the shock and was blinded by the light—something he took, during subsequent psychiatric treatment, to be God's punishment for his drinking on the Sabbath.

A surging mass of boiling debris and gaseous flame, the nuclear blast (left) rumbles across the desert floor just one twentieth of a second after detonation. In the timed sequence below, the pictures taken during the first second (top row) were shot with a telephoto lens, the subsequent ones (bottom row) with a normal lens.

.072 SECOND

.100 SECOND

1 SECOND

8 SECONDS

10 SECONDS

15 SECONDS

Wearing protective boots, Oppenheimer (in white hat) and Groves (center) view the remains at Ground Zero—twisted steel rods that braced the tower.

TREADING CAUTIOUSLY ON SCORCHED EARTH

After the blast, one scientist came in tears to General Groves to report that his instruments had been broken. Groves smiled. "Well, if the instruments couldn't stand it," he said, "it must have been a pretty big bang. And that's what we wanted to know most." In fact, the bang had the force of 17,000 tons of TNT—more than four times the most widely accepted estimate.

Several hours after the explosion, scientists approached Ground Zero in lead-lined armored vehicles to collect soil samples. They found a crater a quarter of a mile across, 25 feet deep at its center and filled with green glass alchemized out of the sand by the intense heat. The tower itself was gone, disintegrated.

Jumbo stands reasonably intact amidst the rubble of its 50-foot tower, 800 feet from Ground Zero.

Like hardened lava, the scorched earth is pocked with heat-fused sand. It bears an emerald glaze that came to be known as ''trinitite,'' or ''pearls of Trinity.''

On July 15, 1945, Harry S. Truman arrived in devastated Berlin for a summit meeting with Winston Churchill and Josef Stalin. There, in the suburb of Potsdam, the Big Three leaders planned to discuss how best to deal with a conquered Germany and a war-shattered Europe. As far as Truman was concerned, however, Europe's future must make room for a higher American priority: ending the war in the Pacific. To that end, the feisty Missourian was determined to get Stalin's commitment to a timetable for the Soviet Union to enter the war against Japan. Truman also intended to use the Potsdam Conference to issue an Allied ultimatum to the Japanese, demanding unconditional surrender.

By the time the presidential DC-4 landed at Gatow Airfield that July day, the countdown for testing the world's first atomic bomb had begun in New Mexico. A successful detonation would give Truman, an avid poker player, a potent hole card to play against both the Japanese and Stalin.

The next day, Truman toured the ruined streets of Berlin. When he returned to the "Little White House"—a rundown villa that had belonged to a German movie producer—Secretary of War Henry Stimson handed him a cryptic cable from George L. Harrison, Stimson's special assistant for atomic energy matters: DIAGNOSIS NOT YET COMPLETE, BUT RESULTS SEEM SATISFACTORY. DR. GROVES PLEASED. Thus did the President learn that the bomb test had been a success. A short time later, Stimson handed Truman a follow-up message from Harrison:

DOCTOR MOST ENTHUSIASTIC AND CONFIDENT THAT THE LITTLE BOY IS AS HUSKY AS HIS BIG BROTHER. THE LIGHT IN HIS EYES DISCERNIBLE FROM HERE TO HIGHHOLD (a reference to Stimson's estate in Long Island) AND I COULD HEAR HIS SCREAMS FROM HERE TO MY FARM.

Truman was elated. With the triumphant test of the Fat Man plutonium bomb and the anticipated success of the still untried "Little Boy" uranium bomb, he could end the War on American terms—without invading Japan or making concessions to Stalin to gain his help against the Japanese. To his aides at Potsdam, Truman referred to the atomic bomb as "the greatest thing in history." It seemed increasingly probable that the President would approve dropping one or more of the bombs on Japan.

Only Japan's acceptance of the unconditional-surrender ultimatum Truman planned to deliver at Potsdam seemed

2

A new President learns his nation's great secret
The search for a German atomic bomb
The decision to spare a city of shrines
A campaign by scientists to withhold the bomb
The search for a face-saving peace formula
Stalin's designs on the Far East
Truman delivers an ultimatum
Prime Minister Suzuki's semantic blunder
"Suggestion approved. Release when ready"

THE PRESIDENT'S ULTIMATUM

likely to stop the President from using the bomb. And a number of factors—among them a curious nuance in semantics—would conspire to make immediate Japanese capitulation on Truman's terms an impossibility.

The man who would write history no matter how he decided had not even heard of the Manhattan Project or the atomic bomb before the awful responsibilities of the presidency were thrust upon him. As F.D.R.'s token running mate during the 1944 campaign, Harry Truman had been told nothing; in his 11 weeks as Vice President, he had met privately with Roosevelt exactly twice, and on neither occasion was he informed of the nation's greatest secret. Only after an accident of fate made him the 33rd President of the United States did Truman learn about what would soon be known as the ultimate weapon.

On the day Truman assumed the presidency, Stimson mentioned to him, almost casually, that the United States had been working for years to develop a weapon of extraordinary power. Even then the War Secretary did not use the words "atomic bomb," for fear of imposing too many pressures at once on the man who, when informed of Roosevelt's death, had groaned, "I'm not big enough for the job."

Not until April 25—as representatives of 51 countries were gathering in San Francisco for the first meeting of a worldwide organization to be known as the United Nations—did Stimson and General Groves give Truman a full briefing on the Manhattan Project. In less than four months, they told him, the United States would test a plutonium bomb. If the detonation was successful, said Stimson, the nation would have "the most terrible weapon ever known in human history." One bomb, Stimson added, could destroy an entire city.

Thus, not quite two weeks into his presidency, Truman was faced with the awesome question of what to do with the power unleashed by the splitting of the atom. No one had ever formulated an official policy. The closest Roosevelt had come was in a meeting with Churchill at Quebec the previous September, when the two leaders had initialed a memorandum calling for an Anglo-American monopoly over "tube alloys," the British code name for the bomb.

After hearing out Groves and Stimson, Truman told the Secretary of War to put together the bluest blue-ribbon committee he could assemble to advise him on the ramifications of the unchained atom and to make recommendations for its future use. A week later, Truman approved Stimson's panel, which was given the innocuous title of Interim Committee. Stimson had selected himself as chairman, Assistant Secretary George Harrison as alternate chairman and six other members: Assistant Secretary of State William L. Clayton; Undersecretary of the Navy Ralph Bard; the Manhattan Project's three administrative scientists, Vannevar Bush, James B. Conant and Karl T. Compton; and James F. Byrnes, former head of the Office of War Mobilization, who would serve as Truman's personal representative.

After several preliminary meetings, the Interim Committee gathered in Stimson's Pentagon office on May 31 for its first full-dress session. General Groves and General George C. Marshall, Army Chief of Staff, also attended, as did physicists Ernest Lawrence, Enrico Fermi, Robert Oppenheimer and Arthur Compton, brother of Karl. Stimson had named the latter four men to a satellite advisory panel to give the Manhattan Project's working scientists a voice in the committee's deliberations.

Stimson opened the meeting by laying out the day's agenda, which was to deal with postwar research and development and international control of atomic weapons. Stimson began by describing the use of atomic energy as "a revolutionary change in the relations of man to the universe," a change, he said, that the United States hoped to use to best advantage. The atom, Stimson added, might help secure world peace or it might mean "the doom of civilization, a Frankenstein that would eat us up."

Stimson then asked the scientists present to discuss the future of atomic weapons. They explained that the first bomb—the one to be tested at Alamogordo—would have a force of somewhere between 2,000 and 20,000 tons of conventional TNT. But within two years, bombs with a force of 50,000 to 100,000 tons of TNT could probably be developed. Lawrence urged that the United States build a stockpile of such bombs after the War in order to maintain a strategic advantage over the Soviet Union.

During lunch, the question of dropping the bomb on Japan came up for the first time. Arthur Compton, who was seated next to Stimson, asked the War Secretary if it would be possible to stage a nonmilitary demonstration of the bomb before employing it against the Japanese. Such a demonstration, he pointed out, might force Japan's leaders to bow to the inevitable and surrender. Stimson decided the matter was worth discussing and called for comments.

Several suggestions for a demonstration explosion were raised, and discarded, for one reason or another. If the Japanese were given advance warning, it was argued, they still had sufficient air power to shoot down the plane carrying the bomb. If the bomb proved to be a dud, the failure would only strengthen the Japanese will to fight on. If a test was made on neutral territory, Japanese leaders might think it had somehow been faked. "Though the possibility of a demonstration that would not destroy human lives was attractive," recalled Arthur Compton, "no one could suggest a way in which it could be made so convincing that it would be likely to stop the War."

With the idea of a demonstration ruled out, Stimson turned the conversation to a discussion of the physical effects that the bomb would have. Oppenheimer said that the visual effects of a nuclear blast would be spectacular—and that it would probably kill 20,000 people within a radius of two thirds of a mile.

Groves added that his engineers and scientists were confident that the new weapon would release a fantastic power; he argued forcefully for its use. "I considered it my duty to recommend that the bomb should be dropped," Groves later recalled. "After all, great numbers of our boys were dying every day." The general bluntly reminded the committee how much money—more than $2 billion—had gone into the bomb. "Our work was extremely costly," he wrote afterward. "As time went on and we poured more and more money and effort into the project, the government became increasingly committed to the ultimate use of the bomb."

The upshot of the Interim Committee's meeting was to recommend to President Truman that the bomb be used without warning against the Japanese, in order to produce maximum psychological shock. The target, the committee suggested, should be "a military installation or war plant surrounded by or adjacent to houses and other buildings most susceptible to damage."

Even before the Interim Committee made its recommendation, General Marshall had ordered Groves to organize a group of scientists and military strategists to evaluate potential targets in Japan. The targets, Groves later wrote, were to be places whose destruction "would most adversely affect the will of the Japanese to continue the War." If possible, the targets were also to be places that had not already been hard hit by air raids, so the damage caused by the atomic bomb could be accurately gauged.

The target committee met several times, and by May 28 it had narrowed its choices to four cities:

Kokura, on the southernmost island of Kyushu, site of one of Japan's largest munitions plants;

Hiroshima, on the main island of Honshu, a major assembly point for convoys of the Japanese Navy, and the site of several war plants;

Niigata, a port on the Sea of Japan that contained a large ironworks, a major oil refinery and a fuel-storage depot;

Kyoto, which had been Japan's capital for more than 1,000 years and was currently the site of several universities and religious shrines as well as numerous war plants.

Groves told Stimson the next day that the targets had been selected and that he was about to take the list to General Marshall. Stimson demanded to see the report immediately. Groves protested that the selection of targets was a

Atomic physicist Arthur Holly Compton wore this badge with a false name at the insistence of General Groves, the Manhattan Project's security-conscious chief. Groves ordered his key scientists to use aliases whenever they traveled; Enrico Fermi became Henry Farmer, and Niels Bohr was known as Nicholas Baker.

military operations matter and that Marshall should see the list first. The Secretary of War replied, "This is a question that I am settling myself. Marshall is not making that decision." When Groves finally read the list of cities to Stimson, he immediately struck Kyoto off the list despite Groves's argument that the city was "large enough in area for us to gain complete knowledge of the effects of an atomic bomb."

Stimson had deeply felt reasons for rejecting such a tempting target. He had visited Kyoto 16 years earlier while serving as governor general of the Philippines and had come away with a keen appreciation of its antiquity and its venerated place in Japanese religion and society. He already was thinking about converting a defeated Japan into the United States's chief postwar ally in Asia, and he was sure that destroying a city as revered as Kyoto would only give rise to a hatred that would smolder among the Japanese for generations. Stimson's reasons did not mollify Groves; as late as the Potsdam Conference, he would be urging the Secretary to put "your pet city" back on the target list. In July, the staff of Major General Curtis E. LeMay's XXI Bomber Command made the port of Nagasaki the fourth target city, and Kyoto was permanently removed from danger.

Like everything else about the Manhattan Project, the deliberations of the target committee and the Interim Committee were classified top secret. But the nuclear scientists were a notoriously independent-minded lot, and before long a fierce debate was raging in laboratories around the country about the decision to drop the bomb without warning.

Sustained and forceful scientific objection to the bomb's use had begun in late 1944 as an unexpected result of an investigation set in motion by General Groves, the weapon's most ardent champion. From the beginning, everyone with knowledge of the Manhattan Project had been driven by a fear, amounting almost to a conviction, that the Germans would develop the bomb first. "We were told day in and day out," recalled one scientist, "that it was our duty to catch up with the Germans." Late in 1943, Groves assembled an investigative task force to follow Allied invasion forces into Europe and assess German progress in atomic research. Groves recruited men for the unit from G-2, the Army's intelligence branch, from Naval intelligence and from the Office of Strategic Services, or OSS. G-2 gave the mission the code name *Alsos*—the Greek word for groves. "My first inclination was to have the mission renamed," General Groves later said, "but I decided that to change it would only call attention to it."

Alsos sleuths first followed U.S. troops into Italy, seeking out scientists in Naples in the hope that they might have some word of German atomic progress. But they learned nothing concrete; the Germans had not taken the Italians into their confidence. After D-Day in 1944, *Alsos* agents trailed Allied columns into France. On August 25 they reached newly liberated Paris, where they searched the intact laboratory of the French nuclear physicist Frédéric Joliot-Curie, whose mother-in-law, Marie Curie, was renowned as the discoverer of radium. Joliot-Curie told *Alsos* agent Moe Berg *(page 63)* that several German scientists had used his cyclotron to smash atoms. From several conversations with them, he confided to Berg, he was sure the Germans were years away from producing an atomic bomb.

Berg and the other agents pushed on in search of more evidence. On November 15, *Alsos* agents reached the French city of Strasbourg, where the Germans reportedly

The 700-year-old Nanzen-ji Buddhist temple presents a picture of tranquillity in wartime Kyoto. The ancient city, famed for its many religious shrines, was removed from the list of possible atomic-bomb targets by United States Secretary of War Henry L. Stimson, who had visited Kyoto before the War.

had centered their atomic research during the Occupation. There the detectives found papers left behind by Carl Friedrich von Weizsäcker, one of Germany's foremost physicists. After studying them, the agents reported to Groves that they were "absolutely certain the Germans did not have an atomic bomb." German nuclear research, they added, was evidently at least two years behind the United States.

Given Germany's head start, such a conclusion seemed incredible. The leaders of the Manhattan Project suspected an elaborate German plot to lull the Allies into a sense of false security. Not until April of 1945, when the *Alsos* men captured and interrogated the elite of German physicists—including Weizsäcker and Nobel Prize winners Werner Heisenberg and Otto Hahn, the man who first split the uranium atom in 1938—were they willing to accept the truth. Nazi Germany had no atomic bomb and had not even tried to build one. The furthest German progress was a small experimental atomic pile that Heisenberg had built in a brewery in the Swabian Alps. Because of a lack of enriched uranium, he had not even been able to start it up.

The news of Heisenberg's failure—combined with the imminent collapse of Hitler's Germany—dramatically altered the assumption under which the Manhattan Project scientists had been laboring: that they had to perfect the bomb before the Germans did, to prevent Hitler from enveloping the world in a nuclear holocaust. Now the only enemy left was Japan—and Japan had neither the resources nor the capacity to build a nuclear weapon. Their *raison d'être* had vanished, and some of them were appalled at the thought of the forces they were about to unleash.

Among the first and most persistent voices to be raised against use of the new weapon was that of Leo Szilard. To the Hungarian-born physicist, the bomb had clearly become a peril to mankind. This represented a total reversal of Szilard's attitude five years earlier, when he had led the effort to alert President Roosevelt to the danger of an atomic weapon in Hitler's hands.

Believing, as before, that the only way to get action was to go to the top, Szilard took almost precisely the same steps he had in 1939. On March 25, 1945, he persuaded Albert Einstein to write Roosevelt a letter warning against precipitous use of the bomb. But when the President died on April 12, the letter from Einstein remained in his desk unread.

Six weeks later, Szilard sought a hearing with the new administration and was directed to James Byrnes, an Interim Committee member rumored to be the next Secretary of State. On May 28—as the targets for the bomb were being selected in Washington—Szilard and two other physicists from the Chicago team, Harold Urey and Walter Bartky, visited Byrnes at his home in Spartanburg, South Carolina.

The meeting accomplished nothing. When the scientists warned against an unrestricted nuclear arms race with the Soviet Union, Byrnes blandly—and mistakenly—replied, "So far as I know, there is not even any uranium to be found in Russia." Moreover, said Byrnes, actual use of the bomb and demonstration of its power were sure to make the Russians more manageable in Europe.

Szilard argued that "the interest of peace would be served and an arms race avoided by keeping the bomb a secret and letting the Russians think that work on it had not succeeded." To a political veteran such as Byrnes, a former senator from South Carolina, the proposal was hopelessly naïve; he pointed out that the country had spent $2 billion on the bomb, and for that Congress would demand results.

Byrnes sent the scientists on their way. The only lasting result of the Spartanburg meeting was Byrnes's disregard for Szilard; thereafter he called the Hungarian "that terrible man." Conversely, the stormy encounter with Byrnes only strengthened Szilard's determination to stop the bomb. Back in Chicago, he joined a committee of seven dissident scientists, headed by Nobel Prize-winning physicist James Franck, who viewed the new weapon as an avatar of doom.

By the second week in June, the committee had completed a document it hoped would restrain the powers in Washington. Its report to the Secretary of War emphasized that the Anglo-American monopoly could not last more than a few years; eventually, the Soviets and the French would also have the bomb. The only possible way to prevent a ruinous arms race, the report contended, was an international agreement rooted in mutual trust. Dropping the bomb on Japan, it insisted, was the worst way to establish any degree of trust. The seven scientists concluded by suggesting that the United States demonstrate the bomb in a desert or on a barren island before representatives of the United Nations—an idea the Interim Committee had already rejected.

Franck took the report to Washington on June 11, hoping to deliver it personally to Stimson, but was told that Stimson was out of town. After some days, the report reached the Interim Committee's panel of scientists. The four men—Arthur Compton, Oppenheimer, Fermi and Lawrence—were asked to comment; they met at Alamogordo on June 16.

"We didn't know beans about the military situation," Oppenheimer later recalled. "We said that we didn't think being scientists especially qualified us to answer this question of how the bomb should be used." As a result, they restricted themselves to recommending that the plea for a bloodless demonstration be rejected. Said Oppenheimer: "We did not think that exploding one of these things as a firecracker over the desert was likely to be very impressive." Ten days later, in one of its final meetings, the Interim Committee in effect ignored the Franck report when it reaffirmed its decision to use the bomb if Japan continued to resist.

Even as the four scientists were discussing the Franck report at Alamogordo, American forces in the Pacific had begun their final assault on Okinawa, the climax of three months of fearsome fighting in which the Japanese defenders had bitterly contested every inch of the island's terrain. When they could hold out no longer, thousands of Japanese soldiers charged suicidally into the American lines. More than 110,000 Japanese and 12,000 Americans died before the battle for Okinawa ended on June 22.

Less than 300 miles away, the Japanese home islands were being ravaged almost daily by hundreds of B-29s, and the Japanese were digging in to repel the expected American invasion. The high command had gathered nearly 10,000 planes of all sorts to employ as Kamikazes when the enemy tried to land. Behind the suicide craft were nearly three million well-rested troops and 28 million civilians who were being trained in the use of primitive weapons in order to make a heroic last stand. Teen-age girls were given woodworking awls and told, "If you don't kill at least one enemy soldier, you don't deserve to die."

But behind the frantic defense preparations and rabid rhetoric, a concerted effort was under way in Japan's highest circles to end the War honorably. To the Japanese, honorable terms meant something short of the unconditional sur-

AMERICA'S BIG-LEAGUE SPY

Catcher Moe Berg of the Chicago White Sox awaits a pitch in 1929. A scout had summed up his abilities tersely as "good field, no hit."

As a professional baseball player, Moe Berg never achieved stardom: In 16 major league seasons he batted only a middling .243. Off the diamond, however, Berg was a man of extraordinary talents, a graduate of Princeton and Columbia Law School who spoke nearly a score of languages. He was to become one of his country's most effective agents in nuclear espionage.

Berg began his spying career in 1934: While touring with a team that starred Babe Ruth, he made movies of Tokyo that eight years later guided the Doolittle raid.

During the War, Berg joined an espionage team assigned to trace German progress in developing an atomic bomb. He followed Allied troops into Italy and in 1944 slipped into Switzerland to attend a lecture by German nuclear scientist Werner Heisenberg. Berg's orders were clear: If Heisenberg's speech even hinted at an atomic bomb, shoot him. He did not have to. The lecture indicated that Germany was years behind the United States.

Early in 1945, Berg scoured western Europe for signs of German nuclear activity. As the War wound down, he became a kidnapper of sorts, conscripting several of Germany's best atomic scientists before the Russians could get them. It was the old ballplayer's most impressive catch.

Agent Berg wears the anonymous black suit and dark tie that he favored as a nuclear investigator for the U.S. government.

A LATE CROP OF DEADLY INTERCEPTORS

With an inventiveness born of desperation, Japanese aircraft designers at war's end developed a range of fascinating new craft intended to counter the Allies' overwhelming superiority in numbers. Some of the planes—such as the Ohka (Cherry Blossom) shown below—were little more than piloted missiles, while others were more sophisticated than anything in the Western arsenal.

The rocket-powered interceptor Shusui (Sword Stroke) at bottom had a fantastic top speed of nearly 560 mph—200 mph faster than the B-29 bombers it was meant to destroy. The versatile Kikka (Orange Blossom) opposite was Japan's first combat jet, and it was intended for a wide spectrum of missions, from suicide bombing to close-support fighting.

Both the Shusui and the Kikka were inspired by the German Messerschmitts that had stung Allied airmen in the last stages of the war in Europe, but the actual execution of the ideas was largely Japanese. The high-performance interceptor Shinden (Magnificent Lightning) at bottom right was a Japanese original from start to finish. The Shinden had its propeller in the rear, a novel configuration that enabled the plane to pack four 30mm cannon into its nose for greater firepower than any comparable aircraft.

Despite the rush to develop them, most of the special planes came too late to help the Japanese cause. Of the four pictured here, only the suicidal Ohka saw combat, claiming its first strike victim, an American destroyer, off Okinawa on April 12, 1945.

YOKOSUKA MXY7 OHKA
The Kamikaze attacker Ohka carried a 2,646-pound warhead in its nose. The standard model with twin fin and rudder, of which some 800 were built, was dropped from a bomber to speed toward its target at up to 600 mph. Plans existed for variants to be catapulted from coastal caves against Allied invaders.

MITSUBISHI J8M1 SHUSUI
The swift little Shusui was designed to rocket to 32,000 feet in little more than three minutes and attack the mighty B-29s with two 30mm cannon in its wings. Then, having jettisoned its undercarriage after takeoff, it was to land on a skilike central skid. However, the engine failed on the Shusui's first test flight and the plane crashed, killing the pilot. No other Shusui ever flew.

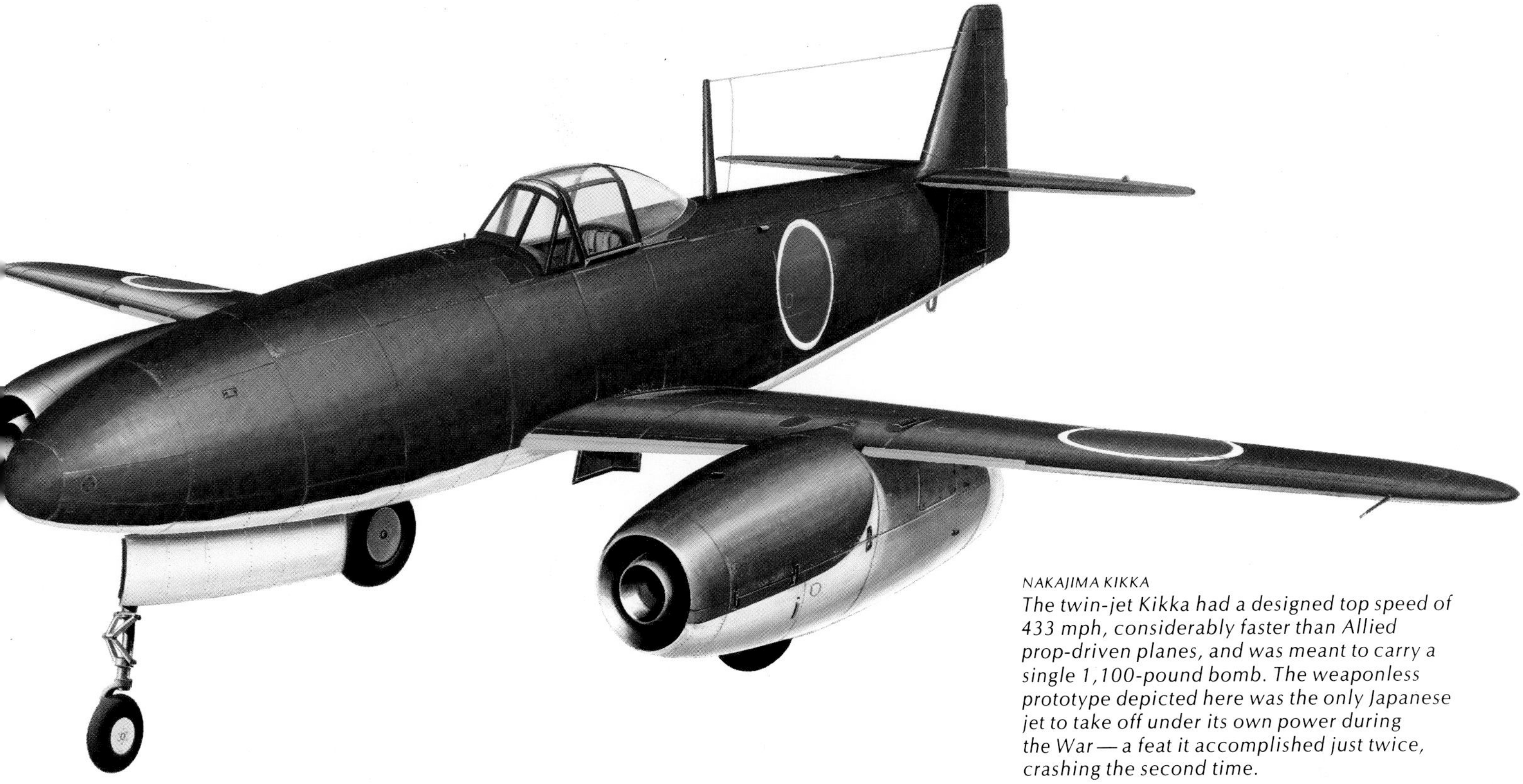

NAKAJIMA KIKKA
The twin-jet Kikka had a designed top speed of 433 mph, considerably faster than Allied prop-driven planes, and was meant to carry a single 1,100-pound bomb. The weaponless prototype depicted here was the only Japanese jet to take off under its own power during the War — a feat it accomplished just twice, crashing the second time.

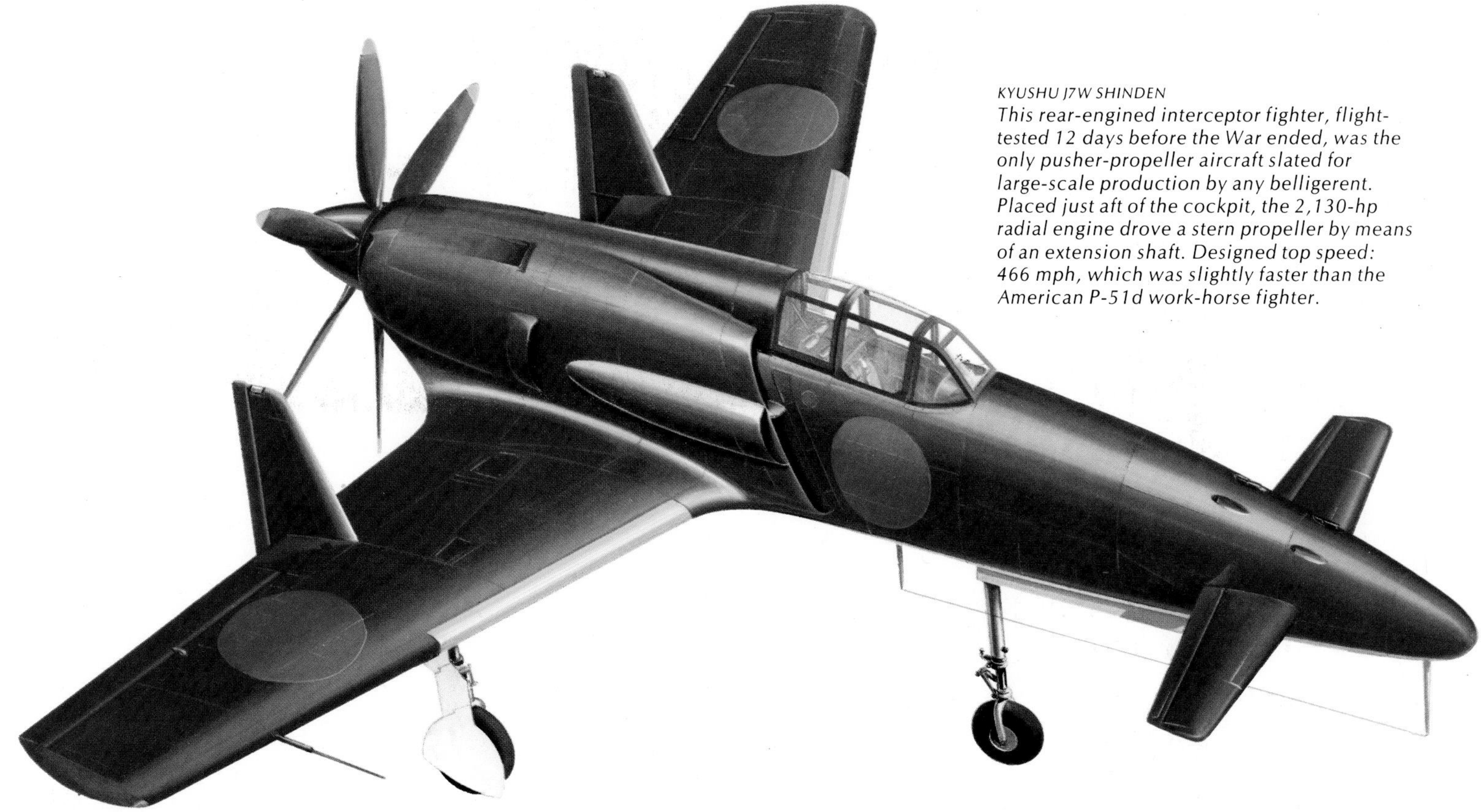

KYUSHU J7W SHINDEN
This rear-engined interceptor fighter, flight-tested 12 days before the War ended, was the only pusher-propeller aircraft slated for large-scale production by any belligerent. Placed just aft of the cockpit, the 2,130-hp radial engine drove a stern propeller by means of an extension shaft. Designed top speed: 466 mph, which was slightly faster than the American P-51d work-horse fighter.

render the United States had been demanding ever since Pearl Harbor. Since the previous summer, individual Japanese diplomats had been quietly putting out peace feelers in Sweden, Switzerland and the Soviet Union, where Japan still had embassies that might open contacts with the West.

For one reason or another, those early feelers had failed to evoke an encouraging response. Then, in April 1945, a move by Stalin caused the Japanese to redouble their peace efforts. The Russians informed Japan that they would not renew the Soviet-Japanese Neutrality Pact when it expired the following year. For the moment, the two countries maintained diplomatic relations, but clearly the U.S.S.R. was preparing to enter the war against Japan. And Japan could not hope to withstand an American invasion with the Russian bear clawing it from behind. Shaken, Prime Minister Kuniaki Koiso resigned. His successor, 78-year-old Baron Kantaro Suzuki, continued to proclaim: "We have no alternative but to fight." Privately, however, Suzuki ordered Foreign Minister Shigenori Togo to seek peace by any means, telling him "as to diplomacy, you have a free hand."

Still, the Japanese were cautious and their signals were often confusing. In early May, Commander Yoshijiro Fujimara, Japan's naval attaché in Berlin, escaped to Switzerland and attempted to open peace negotiations with Allen Dulles, the OSS chief in Bern. But when Fujimara reported his actions to Tokyo, he was warned against "some enemy ruse," and he reluctantly ceased his efforts.

Then on May 12, the subject of peace was unexpectedly brought out in the open at a meeting of the Supreme Council for the Direction of the War. The council included the Prime Minister, Foreign Minister, War Minister, Navy Minister and the Army and Navy Chiefs of Staff, and was known informally as the Big Six. Midway through the session, Admiral Mitsumasa Yonai, the Navy Minister, stunned his colleagues by bluntly suggesting that the Soviet Union be asked to mediate a Japanese treaty with the West. Foreign Minister Togo replied that Yonai was not being realistic, that

the Soviets would soon declare war on Japan. But General Korechika Anami, the War Minister, argued that the Soviets would be approachable because they would prefer a strong Japan as a buffer between the United States and their Asian holdings. Suzuki ordered Togo to draft a memorandum setting a policy for approaching Russia; fearing that General Anami and the Army would contact Stalin on their own if he did not go along, the Foreign Minister reluctantly agreed.

Two days later, on May 14, Togo presented his memorandum to the Supreme Council. "Russia owes her victory over Germany to Japan because we remained neutral," he read. "It would be to the Soviets' advantage to help Japan maintain her international position, since they may have the United States as an enemy in the future."

Togo added a warning that Stalin's price for acting as a peace broker would be "much beyond our imagination"—and would probably include large chunks of Japanese territory. Despite Togo's warning, the Big Six unanimously approved his statement and ordered him to commence negotiations immediately.

That same day, American B-29 bombers boldly raided Nagoya by daylight and razed three square miles of the city. During the next two weeks, the Superfortresses wreaked havoc up and down the home islands, blasting 16 square miles of Tokyo and devastating the city of Yokohama. All this made travel within the home islands perilous and had the effect of delaying the first Japanese approach to the Soviets, whose Ambassador, Jacob A. Malik, was staying at Gohra, a hot-spring resort 70 miles from Tokyo.

At length, Koki Hirota, a prewar Prime Minister and Ambassador to Moscow, was able to travel to Gohra and managed a meeting with Malik, whom he pretended to bump into accidentally while walking through the picturesque mountain village. Over dinner on the evening of June 3, Hirota congratulated the Ambassador on Russia's victory over Germany, adding "It is very fortunate that Japan and the Soviet Union have not exchanged blows in this war." He went on to remark that Japan earnestly desired to renew the nonaggression pact. Hirota also asked Malik if the Soviets would help negotiate a peace with the United States.

Malik was polite but utterly noncommittal during his dinner with Hirota and at a subsequent meeting three weeks later, for Stalin had ordered his diplomats to turn a deaf ear

Allied intelligence personnel, attempting to gauge Germany's nuclear capability, dig for a suspected cache of uranium in a village near Stuttgart in April 1945. In all, the agents seized about 1,200 tons of uranium ore.

to any and all Japanese entreaties. The Soviet dictator reckoned that he was more likely to get a lion's share of spoils from a defeated and helpless Japan than from a country left basically intact through a negotiated peace.

In Washington, American leaders learned of Japan's approaches to Russia—though not from Stalin. Ever since the Army Signal Corps had broken Japan's top-secret diplomatic code in 1940, the United States had been privy to the classified communications of the Tokyo government. Over and over, the same message now appeared as instructions for negotiating were sent to Japanese embassies: "Unconditional surrender is the only obstacle to peace."

That plaintive message made the American command increasingly aware of Japan's darkest fear: that "unconditional surrender" meant loss of the Emperor. To every Japanese, the downfall of Hirohito was unthinkable, for the nation's honor was inseparably bound to the imperial dynasty. Even those Japanese leaders who desired peace would fight to the end in the strongest samurai tradition if they thought the United States might imprison or execute the Emperor.

In late May, several of President Truman's advisers had begun lobbying him to modify the demand for unconditional surrender. They urged him to assure the Japanese that the monarchy would not be abolished and that Hirohito would not be required to face the humiliation of a war-crimes trial. Among those who sought to change Truman's stand were Acting Secretary of State Joseph C. Grew, who had served for 10 years as Ambassador to Japan; Secretary of War Stimson; and Assistant Secretary of War John J. McCloy.

On May 28, Grew sent Truman the draft of a proclamation that he and Eugene H. Dooman, the State Department's leading expert on Japan, had drawn up; it left the way open for retaining the Emperor. "Once the military extremists have been discredited," Grew argued, "the Emperor, purely a symbol, could and possibly would be used by new leaders who will be expected to emerge." Moreover, said Grew, "The Japanese are past masters at executing the maneuver of right-about-face." Hirohito might become a valuable asset in speeding surrender and smoothing the way for American occupation of the home islands.

Truman agreed that Grew's proclamation "seemed a sound idea" and asked him to discuss it with the Joint Chiefs of Staff. Grew presented his argument to the Chiefs the next day. They saw merit in the idea, but pointed out that since the battle on Okinawa was still raging, any American concession might be viewed as a sign of weakness. Grew reported the Joint Chiefs' response to Truman, who told him to shelve the proclamation for the moment.

In the meantime, the new President continued to press publicly for unconditional surrender, well aware that a recent public opinion poll indicated 70 per cent in favor of imprisoning or executing Hirohito. On June 1, in a special message to Congress, Truman reiterated: "The Japanese hope that our desire to see our soldiers and sailors come home again and the temptation to return to the comforts of peace will force us to settle for some compromise short of unconditional surrender. They should know better."

Enrico Fermi (front row, far left) and the scientists who helped build the first nuclear reactor gather at the University of Chicago on December 2, 1946, the fourth anniversary of their success. In 1945, physicist Leo Szilard (middle row, far right) led a spirited protest against using the bomb he had helped to create.

Two weeks later, on June 16, Truman met with the Secretary of War and the Joint Chiefs to discuss strategy for defeating Japan. The central options were continued massive conventional bombing, or a landing on the main islands; neither the atomic bomb nor a diplomatic alternative was on the agenda. But Stimson and Assistant Secretary McCloy planned to revive the idea of permitting the Japanese to retain the Emperor in return for surrender—and threatening to use the atomic bomb if they refused.

At the start of the meeting, Marshall insisted it would be necessary to invade Japan. The first landing, planned for November 1 on the island of Kyushu, would involve 767,600 men; there would be frightful losses, Marshall conceded, but he argued that bombing alone could not subdue the Japanese. Germany had been bombed to rubble, yet had continued to fight until physically overrun by troops.

Stimson, who was suffering from migraine headaches and appeared pale and weak, nodded that Marshall was correct. But the 78-year-old statesman added that the United States should explore alternatives before committing itself—and consigning the Japanese—to the horror of invasion. "There is a large submerged class in Japan who do not favor the present war," Stimson said, adding that "something should be done to arouse them." The Secretary of War stopped short of mentioning the proposal for a negotiated peace.

Admiral William D. Leahy, Chairman of the Joint Chiefs of Staff, was quick to second Stimson. "I fear no menace from Japan in the future, even if we are unsuccessful in forcing an unconditional surrender," Leahy said. "What I do fear is that our insistence on unconditional surrender will only result in making the Japanese more desperate and increase our casualty lists."

Truman appeared to settle the debate by ordering the Joint Chiefs to proceed with plans for the invasion of Kyushu. But then, as the conferees rose, the President turned to the highly respected Assistant Secretary of War: "McCloy, you haven't said anything. What is your view?"

"We should have our heads examined," said McCloy, "if we don't consider a political solution." He then suggested sending a direct message to the Japanese.

"This is just what I wanted considered," said Truman, who had been waiting all along for someone to come straight out with it. "Spell out the message you think we should send."

McCloy, who before the War had been a successful New York trial lawyer, jumped at the chance to argue the proposal he and Stimson had discussed. When he ended with his suggestion to use the atomic bomb if Japan refused to sur-

render, McCloy sensed that "chills ran up and down the spines" of his audience. For the bomb was such a tightly held secret that it was almost never spoken of except as tube alloys, the British phrase, or S-1, the American term.

"That's a good possibility," said Truman, who asked McCloy to draft the message he had proposed, adding, "Don't mention the bomb at this stage." McCloy, Eugene Dooman and Joseph W. Ballantine, director of the State Department's Office of Far Eastern Affairs, immediately began working on the document that later would be known as the Potsdam Proclamation. On July 2, the three men delivered a draft to Truman. It laid out American terms for surrender, including the breakup of Japan's military machine, war-crimes trials and the occupation of Japan. Contained in the document was one vital passage—Article 12—that would allow the Japanese to retain their cherished Emperor:

"The occupying forces of the Allies shall be withdrawn as soon as there has been established a peacefully inclined and responsible government. This may include a constitutional monarchy under the present dynasty if the peace-loving nations can be convinced of the genuine determination of such a government to follow policies of peace."

Truman was impressed by the memorandum, but told McCloy that the warning to Japan "cannot be completed until we know what is to be done with S-1." Doubtless, Truman planned to give the matter more thought on the way to Potsdam. But it appeared that he had softened his attitude enough so that even while demanding unconditional surrender he was agreeing to the one condition that would give the Japanese a way out of the War.

On July 6, Truman boarded the cruiser *Augusta* at Norfolk, Virginia. It was to carry him to Antwerp, Belgium, and from there he would fly to Potsdam to meet with Churchill and Stalin. No one will ever know what agonies of reappraisal Truman underwent during the voyage, or what

discussions he had with James Byrnes, who had been sworn in as Secretary of State on July 3. History records none of it. But sometime during the nine days at sea, Truman decided to eliminate the crucial last sentence of Article 12. Once the altered document was read at Potsdam, the Japanese would have no way to surrender without losing face.

On July 17, Stalin arrived at Truman's Potsdam villa for his first meeting with the new President, who greeted him warmly. Truman had every reason to smile, for the successful test of the plutonium bomb at Alamogordo the previous day meant that he did not need Stalin to fight Japan.

Through his interpreter, Stalin made small talk with Truman and Byrnes, then told them that he had been stalling Japanese peace overtures—a fact the Americans already knew, thanks to their intercepts of Tokyo's cable traffic. Stalin also said that he would attack the Japanese through Manchuria within a matter of weeks.

The next day, July 18, Truman and Churchill met privately for lunch, and the American raised the question of informing the Soviets of the atomic bomb. If Truman told Stalin of the bomb, replied Churchill, the Russian would be angry that he had not been made privy to it much earlier. Truman would have to explain that he had been waiting for its successful test.

Churchill also advised Truman to restore the last sentence of Article 12 and allow Japan to maintain the Emperor. As the British Prime Minister later wrote, it was a matter of finding language "so we all got the essentials for future peace and security, and yet left the Japanese some show of saving their military honor and some assurance of their national existence."

On June 20, another opportunity for a negotiated peace presented itself. Allen Dulles flew to Potsdam to inform Stimson that Japanese officials at the International Trade

Wreathed in smoke, American troops return fire against Japanese positions on Okinawa in May 1945. During the three-month battle to capture the island, the United States lost 12,613 dead and approximately 40,000 wounded—casualties that played a major role in the decision to use the bomb.

Precluded by Japanese militants from making direct contact with the United States, Prime Minister Kantaro Suzuki (left) and Foreign Minister Shigenori Togo appealed to the Soviet Union to mediate a peace.

A NATION FORTIFIED BY KAMIKAZE SPIRIT

Japan planned a nasty reception for American invaders. Everything the nation had left was to be thrown into a last, desperate battle designed to shatter American morale and force the Allies to abandon their demand for unconditional surrender.

Applying the lessons of Saipan and Okinawa—that the enemy must be stopped on the beaches or not at all—construction battalions fortified the shorelines of Kyushu and Honshu with tunnels, bunkers and barbed wire. More than 5,000 planes were rigged for one-way missions and lay camouflaged in coastal meadows or on mountainside ramps—loaded with just enough fuel to reach the invasion beaches. Automobiles were relieved of their engines to power hundreds of suicide launches that would attack American landing craft.

Meanwhile the 28 million women, children and old men in the People's Volunteer Army drilled with bamboo spears and pitchforks, convinced that "strength in the citadel of the spirit" would make up for their primitive weapons. They were joined by another four million well-drilled civil servants and 2.5 million soldiers, many of them brought home from Manchuria and Korea for the "divine chance" to save the Empire—or die trying. If these sacrificial warriors had doubts, they hid them well. "The Imperial Army is confident," boasted one general. "Our men are fortified with the admirable spirit of Kamikaze."

Wielding bamboo spears, village women on Kyushu—Japan's southernmost main island—prepare enthusiastically to repel invaders in April 1945.

Deep within a tunnel that was built for use as a staging base—and a retreat from American bombardment—soldiers drill for the defense of Kyushu. Soldiers and civilians alike were steeled to resist invasion with slogans such as "100 million die together!"

Soldiers, farmers and women in traditional garb build a camouflaged gun emplacement as part of a defense network along Shibushi Bay on Kyushu.

Bank in Switzerland had approached him through a Swedish diplomat named Per Jacobsson. The Japanese bankers had told Jacobsson they would be willing to contact the various peace factions in Tokyo.

But Stimson was too weary and too preoccupied with details of the Potsdam Conference to pay much heed to Dulles. The War Secretary also had doubts about the sincerity of the Japanese approach and their willingness to accept peace on Allied terms. He was more inclined to believe an American intelligence report that insisted "Japanese leaders are now playing for time in the hope that Allied war weariness, Allied disunity or some 'miracle' will present the opportunity to arrange a compromise peace."

Meanwhile, the military men who had accompanied Truman were engaging in their own debate over the bomb. In a meeting with the President on July 22, General Henry "Hap" Arnold, Chief of the Army Air Forces, argued that conventional bombing could easily end the War, despite Marshall's insistence on an invasion. And no less a general than Dwight D. Eisenhower advised that the bomb was "no longer mandatory as a measure to save American lives."

The arguments were academic. By now, Truman had made up his mind. "I regarded the bomb as a military weapon," he later wrote, "and never had any doubt that it should be used." The following day, the President had Byrnes call Stimson, who had returned to Washington, to ask when the first bomb could be used against Japan. Stimson replied next day that it would be ready by August 4 or 5. At lunch, Truman finally took Stalin at least partly into his confidence.

As the luncheon was breaking up, the President walked nonchalantly up to Stalin's interpreter. "Will you tell the Generalissimo," Truman said, "that we have perfected a very powerful explosive which we are going to use against the Japanese and we think it will end the War." Stalin replied coolly. He hoped America would "make good use of it against Japan."

After that brief conversation—during which Truman had scrupulously avoided using the words "nuclear" or "atomic" to describe the weapon—Churchill asked Truman, "How did it go?"

"He never asked a question," the President answered.

Stalin had no reason to question Truman. Soviet intelligence had penetrated the Manhattan Project in 1943; by the time Truman made his deliberately vague remark about the bomb, the Soviets had been working on developing their own nuclear weaponry for two years.

Later that day, July 24, Truman approved an order to be issued by the Joint Chiefs of Staff. It began:

"The Twentieth Air Force will deliver its first special bomb as soon as weather will permit visual bombing after about August 3, 1945, on one of these targets: Hiroshima, Kokura, Niigata or Nagasaki."

On July 25, General Carl "Tooey" Spaatz, who had been appointed commander of Strategic Air Forces for the putative invasion of Japan, received the order in Washington. He immediately left for Guam, where he would brief General LeMay and Colonel Paul W. Tibbets Jr., commander of the 509th Composite Group that was to drop the bomb.

The same day Truman informed Stalin of the bomb, the President and Churchill agreed on the final text of the Potsdam Proclamation. All that was needed to release the document was the approval of China's Generalissimo Chiang Kai-shek. Chiang's assent reached Potsdam on July 26—at the same time that Churchill received word that his Conservative government had been ousted in a general election by Clement Attlee and the British Labor Party.

At 9:20 that night, the Potsdam Proclamation, which threatened "utter devastation of the Japanese homeland" unless Japan surrendered unconditionally, was broadcast worldwide. The Proclamation made no reference to a special weapon, nor did it contain any mention of maintaining the imperial dynasty. The final version of Article 12 said only that "The occupying forces of the Allies shall be withdrawn as soon as there has been established in accordance with the freely expressed will of the Japanese people a peacefully inclined and responsible government."

Tokyo monitors picked up the Proclamation broadcast on the morning of July 27 and rushed a transcript of it to the Cabinet, which was meeting in the Imperial Library. Prime Minister Suzuki and his colleagues painfully scrutinized the Allied demands. Foreign Minister Togo thought he detected some slight leeway for negotiation. But Admiral Soemu Toyoda, the Navy Chief of Staff, demanded an immediate announcement that "the government regarded the declaration as absurd and would not consider it." In the end, the Cabinet agreed that Suzuki would castigate the Proclamation without rejecting it outright. The newspapers would be allowed to print an expurgated version of Truman's words, but would not be allowed to comment on them.

At this point, Suzuki committed a disastrous semantic blunder. At four o'clock in the afternoon he told reporters, "The Potsdam Proclamation, in my opinion, is just a rehash of the Cairo Declaration and the government does not consider it of great importance. We must *mokusatsu* it." The Japanese word *mokusatsu* is written with two ideographs, one of which means "silence" and the other "kill." Literally, then, *mokusatsu* means to kill with silence—but it can also be taken to mean "No comment."

The meaning that Prime Minister Suzuki wished to convey was "no comment"—that the government would continue to study the document but would not make public its conclusions. Most Japanese reporters, however, chose the literal meaning for *mokusatsu*: to kill with silence, or ignore. Their stories were based on their assumption that the government had rejected the Potsdam Proclamation. Several newspapers defied the government order against editorializing. *Mainichi Shimbun* headlined its account "A Laughable Matter." *Asahi Shimbun* said, "Since the joint declaration of America, Britain and Chungking is of no great moment, it will merely serve to reenhance the government's resolve to carry the War forward to a successful conclusion."

Three days later, *The New York Times* decided that Suzuki's remarks did in fact mean that the Japanese had rejected the Proclamation outright; thus the newspaper's lead headline for July 30 was "Japan Officially Turns Down Allied Surrender Ultimatum."

The U.S. government interpreted Suzuki's statement the same way. And so died the last best hope for ending the War without the atomic bomb. On the day the *Times* story appeared, Stimson cabled the President from Washington to request final approval for the order to drop the bomb. In longhand, Truman wrote out his reply for transmission:

"Suggestion approved. Release when ready."

President Harry S. Truman, his back to the camera, turns toward Soviet Generalissimo Josef Stalin as the summit meeting at Potsdam begins on July 17, 1945. British Prime Minister Winston Churchill, at upper left, suggested that Truman lead the opening session of the conference, his first as a member of the Big Three.

THE MAN FROM MISSOURI

Actress Lauren Bacall adorns the piano as newly inaugurated Vice President Harry S. Truman plays the "Missouri Waltz" during a party for servicemen at Washington's National Press Club in February of 1945.

EMERGENCE OF AN UNLIKELY LEADER

No President, it was said, could have been more poorly prepared than Harry S. Truman for the immense burdens of leadership that were thrust upon him in April of 1945. He was lightly regarded by the men around Franklin D. Roosevelt, and there had been little time, and even less inclination, during his brief vice presidency to initiate him into the highest policy-making circles of the Administration.

Harry Truman was, in fact, an easy man to underestimate. In speech and manner, the 60-year-old Missourian was as simple and artless as his small-town upbringing might suggest. He had never attended college, though he had a wide knowledge of American history. As a young man he had tried his hand at farming, with modest success, then at business, with no success at all. At last, deciding on a political career at the age of 37, Truman had entered public office under the banner of a notoriously corrupt political machine.

But though Truman was a Democratic Party regular and loyal to a fault, he proved himself to be strong-minded, diligent and as personally honest as his sponsors were venal. And when he arrived in the U.S. Senate in 1935, he demonstrated both an unexpected breadth of vision and a steely resolve to act on the issues as he saw them. During his first year in Washington, Truman supported Roosevelt's initiative for a law binding the United States to the rulings of the World Court at The Hague—an unpopular cause in a Congress hostile to any international ties. From 1939 onward, he backed the President's controversial efforts to aid countries fighting Germany and Japan. And in 1940, he confounded his border-state constituency by making equality for black Americans an issue in an uphill race for reelection.

Truman was dismayed when fate declared him President; he genuinely had no ambitions for the job. Almost immediately, he was called upon to make momentous decisions, and none more difficult than whether or not to drop the atomic bomb on Japan. To Truman, the course was clear; he made the decision swiftly, aware that although hundreds of thousands of lives might be lost, millions more would be saved by putting an immediate end to the War.

Truman at the age of 15 wears glasses and the bow tie that became his trademark. Severe farsightedness barred him from games and sports.

On their wedding day in 1919, Truman smiles with his childhood sweetheart, Bess Wallace. Her mother claimed that Bess married beneath her station.

SOLDIER, HABERDASHER, COUNTY JUDGE

Harry Truman began a long run of government service in 1905 by enlisting in the Missouri National Guard. Honorably discharged as a corporal in 1911, Truman volunteered when the United States entered World War I and—thanks to some assistance with the eye test from the examining sergeant—was commissioned at the age of 33 a first lieutenant of artillery.

After serving in France and rising to captain, Truman returned home to Missouri; with a friend he became a partner in a Kansas City haberdashery, but the slump of 1921 wiped them out. Through an Army buddy, he sought the backing of the city's Democratic Party boss, Tom Pendergast, and in 1922 won election as an administrative judge of Jackson County, which encompassed Kansas City. He failed to be reelected in 1924 (the only election he ever lost), but two years later he was back in office as presiding judge—in effect, chief executive of the county government.

In spite of his connection with the notorious Pendergast, Judge Truman was never considered anything but a scrupulously honest administrator and an energetic builder of roads and public buildings. His sole deviation from the straight and narrow came in 1934 when he used $36,000 in courthouse-construction funds to erect statues in Kansas City and Independence of Andrew Jackson, his favorite American hero. And everyone forgave him that.

A bespectacled Captain Truman stands proudly in France during the First World War. His cool and resourceful leadership won Truman a wide circle of comrades who later supported him in his political campaigns.

In Independence, Truman looks over papers as an administrative judge, a position that did not require a law degree. The picture behind him is of his mother, Martha.

Solemn amidst the flowers and his smiling fellow judges, Truman takes the oath of office for a second term as presiding judge in 1930.

MR. TRUMAN GOES TO WASHINGTON

In 1934, Harry Truman was facing the end of his second—and by tradition, last—term as a presiding judge. He was 50 years old, and had no prospects. "I thought that retirement on a virtual pension in some minor county office was all that was in store for me," he said. Instead, Boss Pendergast tapped him to run for the U.S. Senate. Helped by his grass-roots connections in every Missouri county, Truman beat two Congressmen in the Democratic primary, then unseated the Republican Senator by a margin of 250,000 votes.

Truman said that he came to the Senate "as timid as a country boy arriving on the campus of a great university." He worked hard, rarely missed a floor vote or a committee session and, perhaps more important to senior senators, he made no grandstanding speeches. Within a few years he had won acceptance to the "club"—the Senate's Democratic insiders.

The onetime county road builder retained his interest in transportation. Truman introduced the bill to create the Civil Aeronautics Authority and investigated the plight of the Depression-stricken railroad industry, which had abandoned 10,000 miles of track, halved its work force and suffered a rash of bankruptcies. Truman traced the problem to Wall Street manipulators, whom he called "The Wrecking Crew," and pushed through reforms in the Transportation Act of 1940.

With his chief political backer Tom Pendergast at his left, freshman Senator Truman joins other party leaders at the 1936 Democratic National Convention in Philadelphia that nominated Franklin D. Roosevelt for a second presidential term.

Senator Truman jauntily descends the Capitol steps in 1940, his sixth year in office. By his own reckoning, he was just then catching on to the Senate's ways.

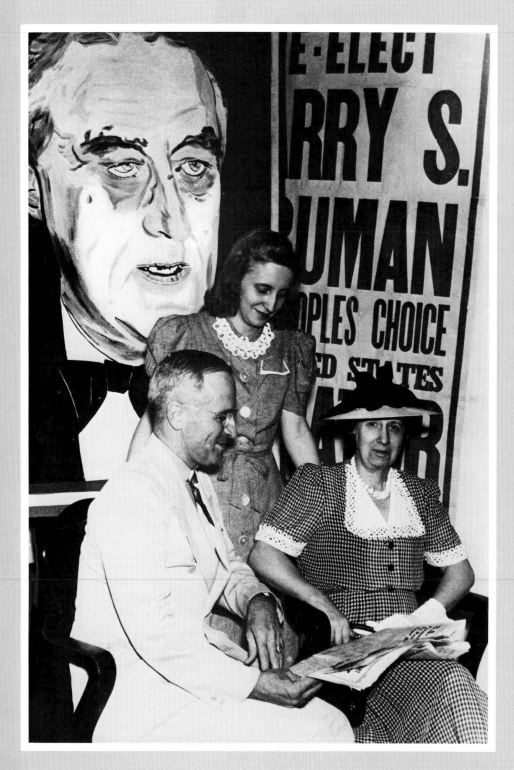

A DOGGED FOE OF WARTIME WASTE

When Harry Truman walked into the Senate after winning reelection in 1940, his colleagues rose in a body to give him a thunderous ovation. As master politicians, they appreciated better than anyone the dimensions of his victory. Missouri's most influential newspapers had been against him; his erstwhile supporter Boss Pendergast had just been convicted of income-tax evasion, and the new leaders of the state Democratic Party had cast Truman aside. But he had campaigned without funds or friends and had overcome all obstacles to take the primary—and go on to win the general election. In the process, he demolished forever the reputation of being "Pendergast's errand boy."

In 1941 Truman proposed a Senate war-investigating committee and was named to the chairmanship. Benefiting from his knowledge of American history, he avoided the mistakes made by a similar committee during the Civil War. He left military decisions to the War and Navy Departments and never tried to make political capital at the expense of the President.

As he traveled to war plants and military bases around the United States, Truman vigorously challenged what he considered waste and inefficiency in wartime spending. At one point he came across the Manhattan Project, but was quietly warned away from what appeared to be a gigantic boondoggle. Overall, the investigations earned Truman a national reputation that led to his choice as a compromise candidate for Vice President in 1944.

Truman, wife Bess and daughter Margaret sit before a 1940 Senate campaign poster and a picture of President Roosevelt, who was seeking a third term. Pressured to withdraw, Truman vowed, "I am going to run for reelection, if the only vote I get is my own."

During a May 1944 hearing, Truman confers with Senators Homer Ferguson (center) and Joseph Ball (right) of the Truman Committee. At this point the watchdog group was investigating a Navy ordnance officer who used restricted data for his own profit.

Truman says good-by to fellow Senators (from left) Homer Ferguson, Harold Burton, Tom Connally and Owen Brewster after resigning the Truman Committee chairmanship to run for Vice President. During his three years of leadership, the committee was credited with saving the government $15 billion.

ELEVATION TO AN EMPTY JOB

Democratic National Chairman Sam Jackson raises Truman's hand in triumph after the Senator's nomination for Vice President in July of 1944. Only Roosevelt's personal plea induced Truman to accept the nomination.

Harry Truman thought the vice presidency a poor trade for his Senate seat. Once in office, he called himself a "political eunuch" and had to make changes in his down-to-earth life style. In a letter to his mother he wrote of a trip to New York: "They send a couple of Secret Service-men along with me nowadays to see that I don't misbehave or do what I choose."

But humor could not displace the apprehension he felt after each of his rare meetings with Roosevelt. They conferred three times after their inauguration in January 1945, and Truman was appalled at the President's deterioration. Though reluctant even to think about the implications of Roosevelt's decline, Truman increasingly worried about his isolation from the inner workings of the Administration—especially in foreign and military affairs.

Margaret Truman reads congratulatory telegrams to her parents after the vice presidential nomination in Chicago. Truman wrote glumly to a friend, "The Vice President simply presides over the Senate and sits around hoping for a funeral."

An ailing Roosevelt lunches with his running mate on the White House terrace in August of 1944. When Truman said he intended to campaign by plane, Roosevelt rejected the idea. "One of us," he said, "has to stay alive."

With his wife and daughter looking on, Truman takes the oath as the 33rd President of the United States. That night he learned for the first time that the United States possessed "a new explosive of incredible power."

FIRST DAYS AT THE SUMMIT OF POWER

Grieving and somber, the new President was sworn into office within three hours after the death of Franklin D. Roosevelt on April 12, 1945. Before the day was out, Truman was coping with the problems of winning the War and solidifying the peace to follow. He announced to the press that the inaugural meeting of the United Nations Organization, set for April 25 in San Francisco, would take place as scheduled.

Germany surrendered to the Allies on May 7, but the U.S. War Department was predicting a cost of 500,000 American dead to invade and defeat Japan. Some put the figure even higher. When the atomic bomb was tested successfully in late July, Truman wrote in his diary, "It may be the fire destruction prophesied after Noah and his fabulous Ark." Even so, he did not hesitate to use it.

A newcomer at the summit, Truman joins Winston Churchill and Josef

Stalin for the Big Three meeting at Potsdam in July 1945. The Americans told Churchill of their atomic progress; Soviet intelligence kept Stalin informed.

3

The heavy cruiser U.S.S. *Indianapolis* had been steaming at high speed across the Pacific for nine days, and now, on July 26, 1945, as the Potsdam Conference was drawing to a close half a world away, Captain Charles McVay brought his warship into the anchorage at Tinian in the Marianas. There he set about off-loading the cargo and the two passengers who had aroused his curiosity ever since leaving Mare Island, California. The passengers wore U.S. Army uniforms and described themselves as artillery officers, but they were oddities—even for Army types. For one thing, one or the other always remained in the cabin they shared, even at mealtimes. For another, if they really were Army officers, why did they wear their artilleryman's crossed-cannon collar insignia upside down?

Then there was the cargo. It consisted of a wooden crate 15 feet long and a monstrously heavy bucket that the unlikely artillerymen had insisted be secured by chains welded to the steel deck of their cabin.

Captain McVay had no idea of the cargo's nature, but it was obviously important. "Every day you save on your voyage will cut the War by just that much," he had been told, so he postponed the en-route training planned for his mostly green crew. And just before sailing he had been ordered to guard the cargo "even after the life of your ship. If she goes down, save the cargo at all costs, in a lifeboat if necessary."

Soon the unloading job was done—after some embarrassment over a winch cable that was six feet too short to lower the heavy bucket into a landing craft waiting to ferry it ashore. Relieved of her mystifying burden, the *Indianapolis* sailed at a more sedate speed for Leyte in the Philippines to begin training for the invasion of Japan. Her crew still speculated that the bucket was probably filled with gold for the purpose of buying Japan out of the War.

Of the 1,200 men on the *Indianapolis,* barely 300 would ever learn the truth—that they had in fact delivered the instrument of Japan's submission. Three days out of Tinian, the *Indianapolis* was cruising along at less than 16 knots when the Japanese submarine *I-58* found and sank her with a spread of torpedoes. Had the bucket still been aboard, no lifeboat or anything else could have saved it, for only a few life rafts and about 800 men remained afloat, and almost 500 of them died in the water before the last survivor was picked up on August 3.

TARGET: HIROSHIMA

Once safely ashore on Tinian, the masquerading artillerymen—actually a Princeton University engineer and a radiologist from General Leslie Groves's Manhattan Project—conveyed the crate and the bucket to the Army Air Forces' huge North Field and left them in a remote, air-conditioned and heavily guarded Quonset hut.

A few days later, Navy Captain William Parsons, the Manhattan Project's chief ordnance officer, unpacked the crate, the bucket, and some equally mysterious containers that had arrived on Tinian by air. Out of the crate came a steel pipe that looked, and would function, like the barrel of a cannon. From another container, Parsons hoisted a cylinder of heavy gray metal with a single hole drilled in its core. And from the lead-lined bucket he plucked a smaller, bullet-shaped plug of the same material—highly refined uranium 235. Fitted together with some of the other components, the three objects would form a deceptively simple-looking device: the first operational atomic bomb.

Parsons attached the uranium cylinder to the muzzle end of the steel gun barrel. Into the breech end he inserted the smaller chunk of U-235 so that, at the proper moment, it would fit precisely into the hole in the cylinder. At that point, the combination would form what physicists called a critical mass—critical, because that many uranium atoms bouncing neutrons off one another would initiate an irreversible and near-instantaneous chain reaction culminating in an explosion that equaled 20,000 tons of TNT.

To join the components and ignite the bomb, a small charge of conventional explosive would be packed into the breech end behind the bullet-shaped piece of U-235, and would be armed with an electrical fuse. Firing the charge would ram the uranium bullet at a speed of 900 feet per second into the uranium cylinder at the muzzle end.

Altogether, with fins and casing and fuse system, the completed bomb was 10 feet long, 28 inches thick and weighed approximately 9,000 pounds. To distinguish it from Fat Man, the spherical plutonium device tested at Alamogordo two weeks earlier, the uranium bomb had been dubbed Little Boy by its Manhattan Project builders.

On Guam, just 120 miles from Tinian, General Tooey Spaatz descended wearily from a transport plane on July 29 after a long flight from Washington, where he had been briefed on his responsibilities as commander of the U.S. Army's new Strategic Air Forces, Pacific. In his briefcase he carried a top-secret order from the War Department, drafted by General Groves, directing the employment of a "special bomb" against Japan as soon after August 3 as weather conditions permitted; he was to drop additional bombs as soon as they could be made ready. The hastily typed document was a reluctant concession by the security-conscious Groves, but Spaatz had insisted on written authority for the moral burden thrust upon him. "If I'm going to kill a hundred thousand people," he growled, "I'm not going to do it on verbal orders. I want a piece of paper."

All the elements necessary for the blow that would bring Japan to her knees had now been assembled within striking distance. Tinian, wrested from the Japanese by American Marines a year earlier, now had four parallel 8,500-foot runways designated VHB—for very heavy bomber. The island was only 1,500 miles from the heart of the Empire, well within the range of the most heavily laden B-29 Superfortress. The latest models of the high-flying Boeing bomber, specially adapted to carry a single large bomb and its monitoring instruments, had been flown in from Wendover Field in Utah by the men of Colonel Paul Tibbets' mysteriously named 509th Composite Group. The first airborne atomic bomb, built at Los Alamos and reassembled at Tinian by Captain Parsons' practiced hands, lay ready in its hut. A second bomb was being assembled nearby as fast as its components arrived.

Wasting no time, General Spaatz shed his flying clothes and summoned Colonel Tibbets and Captain Parsons in order to read them their orders. Present also were Spaatz's chief of staff, Major General Curtis LeMay, and LeMay's operations and meteorological officers. When they heard Spaatz read the words authorizing a strike, the men silently calculated what each of them would have to do.

LeMay, who had masterminded the conventional B-29 bombing campaign against Japan and knew all the strengths and weaknesses of the Japanese war machine, would select the target from among the four cities listed in the directive: Hiroshima, Kokura, Niigata and Nagasaki. Tibbets, the 30-year-old commander of the 509th, would select and lead the crews for the mission; LeMay's operations officer would help Tibbets plan its execution. Parsons was the bomb's midwife, and he would personally see to its loading, arming and delivery. But everything would ultimately depend on the weather officer, who was impatient to get back to his maps and charts and the reports of clandestine weather observers in Japanese-occupied China.

As Spaatz finished reading the directive and returned it to his briefcase, he looked around the table. "Gentlemen," he asked, "are your preparations on schedule?" Each man nodded. The countdown to the fall of Japan had begun.

Back in his own office on Tinian, isolated from the other B-29 commanders, Paul Tibbets turned his attention to the task of drafting the final operations orders and selecting the crews. He had hand-picked the men of the 509th almost a year earlier, and he had been training them ever since in a curious art: releasing a single, exquisitely aimed dummy bomb and then zooming away from the mock target in a maneuver more suited to a fighter plane than to a ponderous four-engined bomber. Not until the last possible moment would Tibbets reveal that the sole purpose of their training was to drop atomic bombs and return alive to report their effects. Now he had a real bomb. Soon he would have a real target.

Tibbets needed seven B-29 crews for the mission. One would fly a backup plane to American-held Iwo Jima and hold it in readiness to take over the bomb and the mission if the lead plane could not proceed beyond that point. Another would go out early to scout the weather over the primary target; two more would scout secondary targets. Two

B-29s would accompany the bombing plane, one carrying a load of instruments to measure the force and effects of the blast, the other a battery of cameras to record it.

To the instrument flight Tibbets assigned one of his best pilots, Major Charles Sweeney, flying a B-29 called *The Great Artiste*. Captain George Marquardt in plane 91, which had no nickname, was assigned to the photo flight. Tibbets had long since decided that he would fly the strike plane himself and would take along his own preferred navigator, Captain Theodore "Dutch" Van Kirk, and bombardier, Major Thomas Ferebee.

After months of practice at Wendover Field, and in Cuba—where part of the 509th had trained for a time— Tibbets knew that Van Kirk seldom missed an estimated time of arrival by more than a few seconds and that Ferebee could consistently drop a bomb within 100 yards of the aiming point, or AP, from 30,000 feet. The strike plane and the rest of its crew would be that of Captain Robert Lewis, a hot-shot pilot from Brooklyn who was fond of reminding his commander that "my crew is the best you've got."

On August 2, Tibbets briefed Ferebee on the mission, and together they made the short hop to Guam to hear directly from General LeMay the choice of their primary target, and two alternates. The cigar-chomping LeMay was almost casual as he led his visitors to a map table and uncovered the charts and reconnaissance photos that were taped to its surface. "Paul," he announced through a cloud of cigar smoke, "the primary's Hiroshima."

LeMay had chosen Hiroshima as the target because he

Jumping-off place for devastating raids against Japan, the 39-square-mile island of Tinian in the western Pacific appears in this aerial photo to be one gigantic U.S. air base. North Field (foreground), headquarters of the 509th Composite Group and numerous other B-29 outfits, boasted four huge parallel runways, each 8,500 feet long.

knew it contained numerous war matériel factories, with the homes of skilled workers packed closely around the plants; it was also the headquarters of the Japanese Second Army, under Field Marshal Shunroku Hata. LeMay believed, incorrectly, that Hiroshima was the only one of the potential targets that did not have an Allied prisoner-of-war camp in the vicinity. He was unaware that Hiroshima Castle, in the center of the city, held at least 23 American prisoners, 13 of them crew members of Okinawa-based B-24 bombers shot down just five days earlier.

Kokura, a previously bombed industrial center and arsenal, and the port city of Nagasaki would be the alternate targets in case clouds prevented Tibbets and his bombardier from seeing their aiming point in Hiroshima. The Joint Chiefs of Staff wanted no mistakes about where the bomb fell; such errors often occurred when bombardiers used radar to pick out cloud-covered targets. And the men who had built the bomb wanted clear pictures of its detonation.

But the focus of Tibbets and LeMay was the primary target, Hiroshima. With Major Ferebee they bent over the photos to find a distinctive ground feature that would provide an unmistakable aiming point, even from 30,000 feet. Ferebee found it first. Leaning past the two men, the bombardier put his finger on a sharply defined T-shaped structure near the center of the several slender peninsulas that made the city resemble an outstretched hand. It was the Aioi Bridge, less than half a mile from Hiroshima Castle. LeMay nodded vigorously, and Tibbets exclaimed, "That's it! It's the most perfect AP I've seen in this whole damn War."

The next day, August 3, LeMay flew to Tinian with a completed copy of Tibbets' order for Special Bombing Mission No. 13—set for August 6. With Tibbets, he disappeared into the heavily guarded hut where Little Boy was resting on a rubber-tire cradle. Soon LeMay departed, leaving the 1,767 men of the 509th with a clear sense that something crucial was about to happen.

It was about time. For too long the members of the 509th had felt like pariahs on Tinian, mostly confined to their own isolated compound, making tame training flights against relatively harmless targets such as the bypassed Japanese garrison on nearby Rota. Only rarely did the crews get an opportunity to make a swift, single-plane swoop over Japan to drop one of the bulbous bombs they called "pumpkins"— training replicas of Fat Man, but packed with conventional high-explosive warheads. For reasons no one explained to them, these missions were never reported in Army communiqués, and so went unnoticed by the fliers of other groups. The regular B-29 crews had to wrestle heavy loads of incendiary and high-explosive bombs into the air night and day and fly them into the teeth of Japanese fighters and flak. They expressed their contempt for the men of the indolent 509th by heaving rocks across the compound fence and scrawling scurrilous graffiti on latrine walls.

So Tibbets' men quietly rejoiced at the signs that something was up, though their taciturn commander offered no explanation for his comings and goings. No individual in the bomb group had ever been told more than he needed to know to do his job. Even now, only Tibbets and a very

At a checkpoint that limited access to the 509th Composite Group's assembly area at North Field, a sentry halts a jeep to verify identification. Only a few senior personnel and technicians given the task of assembling atomic bombs could pass through the gate.

few others knew they were dealing with an atomic bomb.

One privileged insider was First Lieutenant Jacob Beser, a young electronics specialist who had trained for almost a year to monitor Japanese radar impulses and intercept any whose frequency might corrupt the special radar-operated fusing switch built into the bomb. Unless Beser knew exactly what he was doing, the bomb might be triggered miles from its objective.

Beser's responsibility complemented that of Captain Parsons, the graying Navy ordnance officer in overall charge of the uranium bomb. Parsons had worked on the Manhattan Project almost since its inception; he had witnessed the test of the plutonium device in New Mexico, and knew more about the bomb, its fusing system and its explosive potential than any man on Tinian. And he was worried.

One night Parsons had watched four B-29s crash just off the runway during takeoffs for a conventional strike. He knew that a heavy-laden Superfortress was an unstable airplane until it had a lot of air under its wings. And he was haunted by visions of what might happen to the island of Tinian and its 20,000 military personnel if the bomb should explode as the result of a mishap on takeoff.

Parsons carried his concerns to Brigadier General Thomas Farrell, deputy chief of the Manhattan Project, whom General Groves had just sent to Tinian. Together they went over the complex switches in the bomb's fusing system. They were intended to prevent its premature detonation, yet ensure that it would explode when it was meant to.

Three switches were crucial, programed to operate one after another in response to certain circumstances. The first switch would close when the bomb left its bay in the B-29, starting a 15-second timing device that would hold all fusing circuits open until enough time had elapsed for the bomber to begin its getaway turn. A second switch, reacting to barometric pressure, would close at 5,000 feet. The third switch responded to a self-contained radar device that bounced its signal off the ground. At 1,890 feet it would close and set off the explosive charge behind the uranium bullet. There were also conventional fuses in the bomb's nose and tail that would detonate the charge on impact with the ground in case the barometric and radar fuses failed.

Despite the elaborate precautions built into the fusing system, neither Farrell nor Parsons could predict what might happen if the plane bearing the bomb should crash and burn on takeoff. They decided that they would have to send Little Boy aloft without its detonating charge, and that Parsons, who was to accompany it to the target, would insert the charge only after the aircraft was in flight. He would have to perform this intricate task in the cramped confines of the bomb bay, and for that he needed practice.

But first, Parsons had a briefing to give. The men of the 509th Composite Group had waited long enough. Now, in the vernacular of the time and place, they were about to get "the poop from group." On the afternoon of August 4, the crews for the special mission were summoned to the sweltering briefing hut to meet with Tibbets and Parsons.

Tibbets started things off. "The moment has arrived," he said. "Very recently the weapon we are about to deliver

Aircrews who have been selected for the Hiroshima mission receive their preflight briefing from Navy Captain William S. Parsons (left), the bomb's ordnance specialist, and Colonel Paul W. Tibbets Jr., the group commander and pilot of the bombing plane.

A military policeman stands guard while a pair of technicians adjust a canvas screen to conceal the atomic bomb as it is loaded into the forward bay of the Enola Gay.

was successfully tested in the States. We have received orders to drop it on the enemy." Yes, but what kind of a weapon? Captain Parsons took the floor. "The bomb you are going to drop," he said, "is something new in the history of warfare. It is the most destructive ever produced. We think it will knock out everything within a three-mile area." He told the men about the Alamogordo test, about the flash seen 10 miles away, the sound that carried 50 miles and the mushroom cloud that rose 30,000 feet above the New Mexico desert. Then he sat down. No one had yet mentioned the word "atom," nor would they. Little Boy, reposing balefully in its locked and guarded shed, remained an almost total stranger to its wondering escorts.

On August 5 the weathermen confirmed their prediction of fair skies over southern Japan the next day. Little Boy, shrouded with a tarpaulin, was trundled out of the assembly shack to the flight line and lowered into a shallow pit specially prepared to allow ample clearance between the bomb's outsize girth and the low-slung belly of the strike aircraft. With the plane positioned above the pit, crewmen winched the bomb up through the 15-foot bomb-bay doors and shackled it in place.

That afternoon Tibbets handed a scrap of paper to a sign painter, grumpy because he had to leave a softball game, and told him to copy the words on the nose of the plane under the pilot's window. The freshly painted letters read *Enola Gay,* the name of Colonel Tibbets' mother, who had encouraged his boyhood aspirations to become a flier.

A little later, Captain Parsons entered the *Enola Gay* alone, carrying two compact containers. One held pliers, screwdrivers and wrenches, the other a detonator and the bomb's propellant charge. For hours he practiced arming and disarming Little Boy in the close, dark confines of the bomb bay. When he emerged to report his satisfaction to General Farrell, his hands were scraped and bleeding. "For God's sake, man," Farrell protested, "let me loan you a pair of pigskin gloves. They're thin ones." Parsons looked ruefully at his skinned knuckles and shook his head. "I wouldn't dare," he said. "I've got to feel the touch."

Around midnight the crews dined on their choice of some 30 dishes prepared for their send-off. At 1:37 a.m., August 6, the three weather scouts took off, headed for Japan.

Staff Sergeant Wyatt Duzenbury, the *Enola Gay's* flight engineer, was accustomed to spending at least two hours in meticulous preflight inspection of his plane before takeoff. He therefore went aboard early—and unknowingly came within an ace of sending Little Boy to Japan impotent.

As his last act in making certain that everything was ship-shape, Duzenbury crawled into the bomb bay. Carrying a flashlight, he crept along the catwalk on the right side of the bomb, skirted past its nose and returned along the left side. Near the tail of the bomb he kicked and nearly stumbled over two containers lying on the catwalk. These were foreign objects and, so far as he knew, had no business being there. He was kneeling to pick them up and dispose of them when a powerful light flooded through the bomb-bay hatch. Startled, Duzenbury forgot the foreign objects and climbed out to discover the source of all the light. It turned out to be klieg floodlights. General Groves had ordered that this historic occasion should not go unrecorded, and the *Enola Gay* was surrounded by military photographers.

Later, as the full crew climbed aboard, the two strange containers remained undisturbed on the catwalk behind the bomb. They had been placed there during the evening by Captain Parsons, and they contained the tools and the explosive charge he would need to arm the bomb.

Perched on the runway and cleared for takeoff, carrying 12 men, 7,000 gallons of fuel and a four-and-a-half-ton bomb, the *Enola Gay* weighed 150,000 pounds. At 2:45 a.m., Tibbets spoke to copilot Lewis in the right-side seat, saying, "Let's go." Tibbets pushed the throttles, released the brakes, and the *Enola Gay* began to roll. Knowing that he needed plenty of speed to lift the heavily loaded plane, he held it down for all 8,500 feet to the point where the runway ended on the lip of a cliff overlooking the sea. At the last possible second he eased back on the control column and the plane flew. Lewis and Parsons relaxed.

Fifteen minutes out of Tinian, with the plane at about 7,000 feet, Parsons went forward, tapped Tibbets on the shoulder and said, "We're starting." Tibbets nodded, and the Navy captain and his assistant, Second Lieutenant Morris Jeppson, crawled back through the tunnel to the rear compartment and through the hatch into the bomb bay. There, while Jeppson held a flashlight, Parsons went to work on the bomb. It was a delicate and exacting job, requiring 11 successive steps to remove the gun breech behind the uranium bullet, insert the explosive charge, replace the breech and hook up the firing circuits. The job took about 20 minutes. The two men crawled out again and took up vigil at a console whose colored lights would monitor the bomb's interior condition until it dropped.

About 4:30 a.m. Tibbets turned over the wheel to copilot Lewis and crawled through the tunnel to have a look at his aircraft and its crew. In the rear compartment he found four men including Technical Sergeant George Robert Caron, the tail gunner who needed to be at his post only over the target. "Bob, have you figured out what we are doing this morning?" Tibbets asked. At the briefing he had described the bomb in general terms, but this was the first time he had invited speculation about its top-secret nature.

"Colonel, I don't want to get put up against a wall and shot," the gunner said nervously.

Tibbets grinned at him. "We're on the way now. You can talk."

"Are we carrying a chemist's nightmare?" Caron asked.

"No. Not exactly."

"How about a physicist's nightmare?"

"Yes."

Tibbets stuck his head and shoulders into the tunnel and prepared to crawl back forward, but Caron reached in and tugged at a leg.

Ready to launch the Enola Gay are Lieut. Colonel John Porter, the ground operations officer (standing, left), and the crew. Standing are Captain Theodore Van Kirk, Major Thomas Ferebee, Colonel Paul Tibbets, Captain Robert Lewis and First Lieutenant Jacob Beser. Kneeling (from left) are Sergeant Joseph Stiborik, radar operator; Sergeant George Caron, tail gunner; Private First Class Richard Nelson, radioman; Sergeant Robert Shumard, assistant engineer; and Sergeant Wyatt Duzenbury, flight engineer. Not shown are the bomb's special handlers, Captain William Parsons and Second Lieutenant Morris Jeppson.

"What's the problem?" Tibbets asked, looking over his shoulder.

"No problem, Colonel. Just a question: Are we splitting atoms?"

Tibbets stared at the gunner, turned and crawled up the tunnel. He still was not ready to use that word. Nor was he prepared to share with anyone but Parsons the fact that he carried cyanide capsules to be offered to the crew for their discretionary use in case they were captured.

At 5:05 a.m. the three planes that would fly to Hiroshima assembled in a loose V-formation over Iwo Jima and bore northwestward toward the home islands. On the ground, the crew of the stand-by B-29 watched them go and relaxed. They would not be needed this day.

At about 6 a.m., Jacob Beser, the *Enola Gay's* electronics specialist, was monitoring his instruments and got an unpleasant surprise. On his screen he could read the sweep of Japanese radar, operating at the outer limit of its range, and he knew when it stopped its restless searching that it had momentarily locked on to the *Enola Gay*. So now they were expected. Beser kept the knowledge to himself, believing it would serve no purpose to worry the rest of the crew; he did not even tell Tibbets. Half an hour later, Jeppson climbed into the bomb bay again, took three green plugs from the bomb casing and replaced them with red plugs. Little Boy was now not only armed; it was alive and ready to go.

When Jeppson reported to him, Tibbets decided that the time had finally come to speak the forbidden word. He switched on the intercom and spoke. "We are carrying the world's first atomic bomb," he said in a matter-of-fact tone. "When the bomb is dropped," he went on, "Lieutenant Beser will record our reactions. This recording is for history, so watch your language." He spoke again for Caron's ears. "Bob, you are right. We are splitting atoms. Now get back to your turret. We're going to start climbing."

At 7:09 a.m., Radio Hiroshima broadcast an air-raid alert. The alarm warned of the approach of a B-29 called the *Straight Flush,* flown by Captain Claude Eatherly. This was the weather scout; it carried no bombs. Eatherly was delighted to find the sky over the city almost clear, and at 7:24 he got off a report, "Cloud cover less than three tenths all altitudes. Advice: bomb primary." Eatherly turned toward

home, and at 7:31 a.m. the all clear sounded in Hiroshima.

More than 100 miles to the south, Tibbets, once more in the pilot's seat, glanced at the radio operator's copy of Eatherly's message and said, "It's Hiroshima." Half an hour later the navigator, Van Kirk, announced: "Ten minutes to AP"—the aiming point on Aioi Bridge. Van Kirk called a final slight change to a heading of 264°, a little south of due west. The *Enola Gay* droned on at 31,060 feet, with an indicated air speed of 200 miles per hour. At 8:12 a.m. Van Kirk called, "IP." They had reached the initial point of the bombing run. Ferebee leaned his forehead against the headrest that had been made to keep him steady above the Norden bombsight. Tibbets called, "On glasses." Everybody in the plane except Tibbets, Ferebee and Beser, who most needed to see what they were about, pulled down polarized black goggles from their foreheads to protect their eyes.

Below, at 8:13 a.m., a watch station 19 miles east of the city reported three B-29s coming in; radar had apparently lost the planes, and they went unreported until ground observers spotted them; one minute later the alert reached Radio Hiroshima. Aloft in the *Enola Gay*, the chronometer read 08:14:45 when Ferebee announced to the crew that the city was coming up in his bombsight. Beser advised Parsons that no Japanese radar was on a frequency likely to bother his bomb. Ferebee said, "I've got it," and switched

A moment before takeoff from Tinian, Colonel Tibbets waves from the pilot's seat of the floodlit Enola Gay. In order to gain maximum ground speed, Tibbets took the airplane so close to the end of the runway that his alarmed copilot almost snatched at the controls to pull it up.

on an automatic synchronizer that gave him control of the last 15 seconds of flight before the bomb was released. A tone signal sounded in the crewmen's earphones; when it stopped the bomb would be gone.

The tone ceased at precisely 08:15:17. Ferebee yelled, "Bomb away!" Tibbets shoved the throttles forward, swung the wheel and pushed it ahead to throw the *Enola Gay* into the violent, right-hand, 155-degree diving turn designed to take the plane beyond Little Boy's monstrous grasp.

Forty-three seconds after the bomb dropped out of the *Enola Gay's* belly, and nearly six miles below the speeding aircraft, the third switch tripped obediently. A pinkish, purplish flash appeared, and grew, and grew, and grew.

Aboard the *Enola Gay* the flash lighted up instrument faces until they seemed to glare. To Tibbets, the light seemed to have substance. "It tasted like lead," he remembered later. To Caron, alone in his grandstand seat in the tail turret, the sight was terrifying. A great, gray ball of air, compressed until it had become visible, was rushing up at the plane. Caron tried to yell a warning but his voice made only noise. Then the shock wave hit, and the men inside the plane were tossed about like dolls. To Tibbets it felt like an antiaircraft burst and he yelled, "Flak!" Ferebee shouted, "The sons of bitches are shooting at us!" By now Caron had regained control of his larynx, and screamed, "There's another one coming!" The second shock rammed them and passed on, and the *Enola Gay* flew in quiet air.

Beser picked himself up, switched on his recorder and prepared to take testimony from the crew. From his seat in the tail, Caron reported, "A column of smoke rising fast. It has a fiery red core. A bubbling mass, purple-gray in color, with that red core. It's all turbulent. Fires are springing up everywhere, like flames shooting out of a huge bed of coals. . . . Here it comes, the mushroom shape that Captain Parsons spoke about. It's like a mass of bubbling molasses. . . . It's nearly level with us and climbing. It's very black but there is a purplish tint to the cloud. The city must be below that. . . ." So it was—what was left of it.

At 2:58 p.m. the *Enola Gay* landed on Tinian. General Spaatz was waiting, along with several thousand others. As soon as Tibbets climbed down from the hatch, the general strode forward and pinned the Distinguished Service Cross on his flight suit. Aboard the cruiser *Augusta*, en route home from Potsdam, President Truman got the word by radio.

In the United States, on the eastern side of the international date line, it was still August 5 when the bomb detonated. General Groves received the strike signal in his Washington office just before midnight, and General George Marshall was informed. Groves spent the night on an Army cot, waiting for the more detailed report he received from General Farrell about 4:30 a.m. on August 6. At dawn he took the report to Marshall, who telephoned Secretary of War Henry Stimson via scrambler at his home on Long Island. The two agreed to release a presidential statement previously prepared for this moment. Carried across the United States by commercial radio, and to Japan by government short-wave transmitters, Truman's statement said in part: "It is an atomic bomb. It is harnessing the basic power of the universe. The force from which the sun draws its power has been loosed upon those who brought war to the Far East. . . .

"It was to spare the Japanese people from utter destruction that the ultimatum of July 26 was issued at Potsdam," Truman's message continued. "Their leaders promptly re-

The 509th Composite Group crowds around the Enola Gay after its return from Hiroshima. While the flight was in progress, the entire unit was finally let in on the secret of the mission.

Aerial photographs of Hiroshima before and after August 6 attest to the bomb's devastating effect. An X marks the approximate drop point, or Ground Zero; the circles indicate 1,000-foot intervals. The intended aiming point was the T-shaped Aioi Bridge, visible at the upper left of the inner circle.

jected that ultimatum. If they do not now accept our terms they may expect a rain of ruin from the air, the like of which has never been seen on this earth.''

In Tokyo, the first high official to hear of Truman's pronouncement was Chief Cabinet Secretary Hisatsune Sakomizu. He was in bed and half asleep when the Domei News Agency telephoned. Here, Sakomizu thought, was ''the golden opportunity'' to get out of the War with grace. He telephoned Prime Minister Kantaro Suzuki. Then the Lord Keeper of the Privy Seal, Marquis Koichi Kido, was informed. Kido, in turn, reported the news directly to the Emperor. Hirohito was aghast. ''We must bow to the inevitable,'' he said. ''No matter what happens to me, we must put an end to the War as soon as possible.''

But no response came from the Japanese government. For all the veneration accorded him by the people, tradition gave the Emperor no more political power than an icon. Only the Cabinet could end the conflict, and it had been unable to agree on the circumstances for doing so.

The bombing of Hiroshima did nothing immediately to break the Cabinet's long and bitter stalemate. When Prime Minister Suzuki summoned its members the next day, Foreign Minister Togo again argued for acceptance of the Potsdam terms, declaring that the atomic bomb ''drastically alters the whole military situation and offers the military ample grounds for ending the War.'' But the Army, holding out for a suicidal last-ditch battle on home soil, remained

adamant. War Minister Korechika Anami declared that a move toward peace was uncalled for. ''Furthermore,'' he said, ''we do not yet know if the bomb was atomic.'' It could be an American trick, Anami warned; after all, the government had no proof, nothing but Truman's word for it.

The most Anami would agree to was to send Yoshio Nishina, Japan's most distinguished nuclear physicist, to Hiroshima to investigate and submit an opinion. The scientist was to be accompanied by Lieut. General Seizo Arisue, the Army's chief of intelligence, but because of an air-raid alarm, Arisue flew alone to Hiroshima a day ahead of Nishina. His plane arrived at dusk over a spectacle so bewildering that the pilot was unsure where he was. Arisue stepped down from the aircraft onto what at first seemed a barren plain—no voices, no fires, no movement, unlike any bombed city he had ever seen. When a lieutenant colonel came to meet the general and saluted, Arisue saw that the left half of the man's face was badly burned.

The colonel took Arisue by motorboat to a dock where he met an old friend from military academy days, Lieut. General Hideo Baba of the Army's Maritime Transport Command. His daughter, Baba said, had been killed on her way to high school that day. ''Not my daughter alone, but thousands of other innocent children were massacred. This new bomb is satanic, too atrocious and horrible to use.''

Nishina arrived in Hiroshima the next day and had no difficulty deciding that an atomic bomb had exploded; urani-

um, he guessed, had been used—the same strange metal he himself had been experimenting with for years. He asked Arisue whether he ought to go on with his nuclear research. The general let the question go unanswered.

But Nishina's expert report was not enough. The militarists in the Japanese Cabinet could not bring themselves to budge. Nor would they confide in the people. Newspapers and the radio were permitted only to speak vaguely of a "new type" of bomb and of "extensive damage" inflicted on Hiroshima by a few planes.

In only one direction was there movement. A note of desperation sounded in the message that Foreign Minister Togo sent to Ambassador Naotake Sato in Moscow: THE SITUATION IS BECOMING SO ACUTE THAT WE MUST HAVE CLARIFICATION OF THE SOVIET ATTITUDE AS SOON AS POSSIBLE. PLEASE MAKE FURTHER EFFORTS TO OBTAIN A REPLY IMMEDIATELY.

Resignedly, Sato turned to the telephone. For weeks he had been trying to tell the Tokyo government as bluntly as diplomatic *politesse* would permit that Moscow had no interest in either mediating an end to the War or renewing the Soviet-Japanese Neutrality Pact that still had almost a year to run. Sato did not expect to have much better luck this time, but even so he was not prepared for the response.

Curiously, the office of Foreign Minister Vyacheslav M. Molotov promptly offered the Japanese Ambassador an appointment for 8 p.m. on August 8. Lately Molotov had been ignoring Sato's calls or putting him off with excuses. Sato was even more surprised when, early in the afternoon, he received a call moving the appointment up to 5 p.m.

When Sato appeared at the Kremlin, Molotov admitted him at once. He brusquely waved aside the Ambassador's formal greeting in Russian and said, "I have here, in the name of the Soviet Union, a notification to the Japanese government which I wish to communicate to you."

Sato took a chair indicated by Molotov, who seated himself at a long table and began to read: "After the defeat and capitulation of Germany, Japan remains the only great power which still stands for continuation of the War." The statement continued through four paragraphs of explanation, mainly citing Russia's sacred duties to its allies. "In view of the above," it concluded, "the Soviet government declares that from tomorrow, that is from August 9, the Soviet Union will consider itself in a state of war with Japan."

Knowing that protest would be useless and that the only asset he had left was his personal dignity, Sato politely made his exit. He took with him Molotov's assurance of high personal regard and the promise that he could send

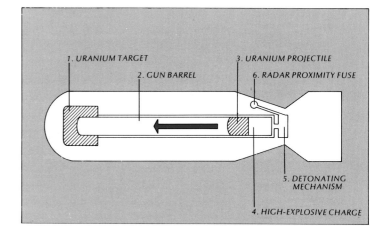

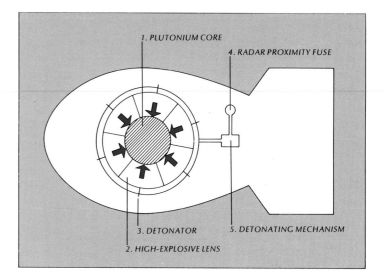

any cables he wished, in code if he so desired. But when Sato got back to the Embassy he found his telephones already disconnected and his radio equipment confiscated. The messages he tried to send commercially somehow never got past the cable office. Two hours after Sato left Molotov, 1.6 million Soviet troops crashed across the Manchurian border to take on Japan's Kwantung Army. But that once-feared and renowned force had become a mere shadow of itself, shrunk by the demands of other theaters to little more than 600,000 green and ill-armed troops.

On the same day as the meeting in Molotov's office, the first of many reconnaissance photos of what had been done to Hiroshima arrived in Washington. They provoked intense discussion at the highest levels of government. Admiral Leahy, Chairman of the Joint Chiefs of Staff, was shocked to his core; he called the atomic weapon inhuman, and voiced his opinion that by using it the United States had "adopted an ethical standard common to the barbarians of the Dark Ages." War Secretary Stimson was similarly distressed and concerned about what would happen next, even though, all along, he had favored using the bomb. Stimson thought the time had come for a softer approach to the Japanese. "If you punish your dog, you don't keep souring on him all day after the punishment is over," he said. "If you want to keep

his affection, punishment takes care of itself. It's the same way with Japan. They naturally are a smiling people and we have to get on those terms with them."

As he had before, President Truman disagreed. He said he recognized his "terrible responsibility" for the suffering implicit in the photographs, but the Japanese had not surrendered or even hinted at surrender. And they had been warned. Unless he intervened, Truman reminded his advisers, a second bomb was scheduled for delivery on August 9, and then a third and a fourth as soon as their components could be rushed to Tinian.

The second bomb resembled the Hiroshima bomb only in its three-switch fusing system and its potential for havoc. Bulkier than the first, it was approximately 5 feet thick at the waistline and 10 feet 8 inches long. Instead of uranium 235, the heart of this bomb was a ball of plutonium, and instead of a device for firing one chunk of fissionable material down a gun barrel into another chunk, the mass of plutonium would be forced to go critical by the simultaneous compression of 64 exploding "lenses" arranged around the sphere. The new weapon was called Fat Man, and there was little reason to doubt that it would work: Its prototype was the bomb of the same name tested at Alamogordo.

To deliver Fat Man, Colonel Tibbets chose Major Charles Sweeney, who had flown the instrument plane on the first mission. Because Sweeney's plane was still crammed with instruments, he borrowed Captain Frederick Bock's plane, known as Bock's Car. The only man from the Enola Gay assigned to fly in the bombing plane again was Lieutenant Beser, the radar specialist.

Tibbets and his crew had done a technically near-perfect job at Hiroshima. Sweeney was determined to prove that he could perform just as smoothly. But it was not to be; the Bock's Car mission seemed jinxed from the start.

It was after 2 a.m. on August 9, and the strike plane with Fat Man in the bomb bay was on the hardstand being prepared for takeoff. As the crew stood talking, Sergeant John Kuharek, the flight engineer, reported the first bad news. A fuel-transfer pump had broken down; 600 gallons of gasoline were trapped in a bomb-bay reserve tank and could not be fed to the engines. Tibbets and Sweeney talked the problem over. If they delayed the flight, the weather might go

The uranium-cored "Little Boy," its casing opened for inspection, rests on a dolly used to move the bomb from its assembly shed to the loading pit beneath the Enola Gay. The schematic representation of the bomb's interior shows how the two pieces of uranium necessary to form a critical mass were brought together. The larger piece (1), affixed to the muzzle end of a six-foot gun barrel (2), was cupped in the center to receive a second piece (3) that was propelled down the gun barrel by an explosive charge (4) acting like the powder in a shotgun shell. The explosive was detonated by an electrical mechanism (5) triggered by a radar-operated proximity fuse (6) that continuously measured the distance to the ground and initiated an electrical impulse at 1,890 feet.

The "Fat Man" plutonium bomb bears signatures and messages scrawled by aircrewmen and technicians at Tinian. The diagram shows how the triggering mechanism differed from the less sophisticated, gunlike device employed at Hiroshima. A radioactive core of two joined hemispheres of plutonium (1) was surrounded by an array of centrally focused explosive "lenses" (2) to which electrical detonators (3) were attached. A radar proximity fuse (4) activated an electrical device (5) that detonated the explosive lenses simultaneously, crushing the plutonium ball inward and compressing it into the critical mass necessary for an atomic explosion. The artist's conceptions shown here, though derived from authoritative descriptions, are only approximate; details of the bombs' inner workings remain zealously guarded secrets.

sour. But if they went ahead they risked running short of fuel. Sweeney decided to go, trusting that he could find an emergency roost on Iwo Jima or Okinawa.

The bomb's Manhattan Project escort was Navy Commander Frederick Ashworth, but his duties were somewhat simpler than Parsons' had been on the earlier flight. With 64 different, precisely timed explosive charges inside the casing, arming the bomb could not be accomplished in the bomb bay. Fat Man went down the runway fully armed.

The takeoff was perfect. At 3:49 a.m., *Bock's Car* was climbing toward cruising altitude. The primary target was the arsenal city of Kokura on the southern island of Kyushu. Nagasaki, the shipbuilding and torpedo-factory center 100 miles to the southwest, was the secondary target. Sweeney would know which to hit when the weather planes reported from far ahead. The crew's orders were to bomb visually—not by radar, but "by naked eye or scratch." If they could not see their AP clearly, they were to abort the mission and either land with their unwieldy and unpredictable weapon still on board or jettison it in the ocean.

At 7 a.m. the *Bock's Car's* apparent jinx began to assert itself in a terrifying manner. Ashworth's assistant, Lieutenant Philip Barnes, was watching the black-box console that monitored Fat Man's entrails. Ashworth dozed beside him. Suddenly Barnes croaked, "Look!" and Ashworth sat up. A red light on the box that should have been blinking on and off with metronomic regularity had begun to fibrillate like a stricken heart. At worst, this could mean that the bomb would go off in a matter of seconds. At best, whatever had gone awry was confined to the console's complex circuitry.

Within seconds, Barnes had the cover off the box and his trained fingers were tracing out the wiring. Two switches had somehow been set in reversed position. Ashworth went forward to tell Sweeney, who merely breathed, "Oh, Lord!"

Real trouble set in at 8:40 a.m., when Sweeney reached the rendezvous point over Yaku-shima off the coast of Kyushu. There at 31,000 feet the photo and instrument planes were to join up, and the three would proceed together from the small island to the primary target. *The Great Artiste*, carrying the instruments again, came up promptly and waggled its wings. But minutes dragged by without any sign of the photo plane, whose pilot was making a wider circle of the area at a higher altitude. Sweeney could not call the plane by radio, for the mission was enjoined to strict radio silence.

Now the fuel gauges became a critical factor. During its climb, lugging Fat Man up to 31,000 feet, *Bock's Car* had been burning fuel at a rate of 1,000 gallons per hour. Sweeney circled for a dangerous 45 minutes. Then, reluctantly, he wheeled away for Kokura, where the weather plane had reported that the sky was clear.

At 9:50 *Bock's Car* was at the initial point and turning for Kokura. Clouds had begun to move in since the weather plane's survey, but the city was still visible through the broken undercast. "What do you think, Bea?" Sweeney called to the bombardier, Captain Kermit Beahan.

"Shouldn't be any trouble, Chuck," Beahan answered, but a minute later he swore, "Damn it, damn it to hell!" The aiming point, downwind from a smoldering city nearby that had been hit two days earlier in a conventional raid, was obscured under drifting smoke. Sweeney spoke into his mike, "Pilot to crew. No drop."

They tried another run. Still the smoke masked the target and there was no drop. Both Beahan and the tail gunner reported flak stepping up to their level and closing from behind. Then Beser reported hearing conversations on the Japanese fighter-control radio frequency. The fighters did not worry Sweeney; he doubted they could reach his altitude in time to catch him. But the flak could be something else.

Sweeney tried a third run, this time from another direc-

A mushroom-shaped cloud boils up over Nagasaki as superheated air from the atomic fireball condenses in cooler layers of the atmosphere. The pillar of steam, dust and ash rose more than 12 miles above the earth.

tion, but the devilish smoke was still there, cutting off vision at least a mile short of the aiming point. By now the flak bursts were close enough to make the plane buck. One crewman muttered: "Let's get the hell out of here!"

Flight Engineer Kuharek spoke up on the intercom. Fuel was critically low, considering how far they were from home. They would not be getting back to Tinian in any case; it was Iwo Jima, Okinawa or ditch.

Sweeney and Ashworth conferred. They could not stay over Kokura any longer. How about a try at Nagasaki? They agreed and Sweeney swung *Bock's Car* to the southwest, trailed by *The Great Artiste*. Nagasaki had one cardinal virtue: It was on the way to Okinawa.

Gloom settled on the crew as they came up on Nagasaki; the city was under seven tenths cloud cover. Beahan, the bombardier, could make out the docks and the general outlines of the city, but the aiming point, the Mitsubishi arms complex, was out of sight.

"We can make only one run," Sweeney told Ashworth, "and Beahan doesn't think he can get a visual fix. I suggest we drop by radar. What do you think?" Sweeney commanded the plane, but Ashworth, in charge of the bomb and coleader of the mission, had to concur in all decisions.

"I don't know. Let me think about it," Ashworth said. He was worried; the usual-bombing order had been specific.

"Anything is better than dumping it in the ocean," said Sweeney pointedly, thinking of Fat Man's $25-million price tag. "I have a lot of confidence in my radar and I will take the responsibility."

Reluctantly, Ashworth agreed. Then, as they came up on the target, a hole opened in the clouds and Beahan yelled, "I've got it! I see the city. I'll take it now."

Fat Man fell at 11:01 a.m., and was due to explode slightly less than a minute later at 1,500 feet. Relieved of its weight, *Bock's Car* leaped upward and Sweeney threw the aircraft into the high-speed getaway turn. For a while he was afraid he had dropped a dud. It seemed at least two minutes must have passed since Beahan's shout of "Bombs away!" and his sheepish correction a second later, "Bomb away." But then the great flash came, and shortly thereafter *Bock's Car* was hammered by five successive shock waves from the mountains and valleys around Nagasaki.

Staring out at the tumbling mushroom cloud, a crewman spoke to the radio operator. "How do you feel now?"

"Would you mind shutting up?" the radioman snarled.

"I feel the same way. Only worse," the gunner said.

In spite of his dwindling fuel supply, Sweeney decided to fly a complete circle around the city and use up 12 precious minutes collecting visual observations before straightening away for Okinawa along with *The Great Artiste*. Within half an hour the "lost" photo plane, observing the blast, flew over Nagasaki and then headed toward Okinawa, knowing that the mission had been accomplished.

The gauges said that *Bock's Car* had scarcely 300 gallons of fuel remaining in its tanks. Normally the aircraft burned that much in an hour, if lightly loaded and going downhill. Sweeney was sure they would have to ditch. He tried raising the Navy's air-sea rescue units. No response. The flying boats and submarines, assuming that the mission was long since finished, had secured and left their stations.

Engineer Kuharek nursed his four Wright Cyclone engines to save every drop of gas. At last, as the crew's hopes faded, Okinawa came up on the radar screen, then appeared on the horizon. Kuharek spoke: "Skipper, as of right now, the gauges read empty." Simultaneously the right outboard engine began to cough. Then it died.

Okinawa's Yontan airfield came in view, but to Sweeney's dismay it was jammed with traffic, planes taking off and landing. The tower did not answer *Bock's Car's* frantic calls of "Mayday! Mayday!"

"Fire the flares!" Sweeney yelled.

"Which ones?"

"Fire them all. Every goddamn one!"

Twenty flares, an aerial Fourth of July demonstration, burst from the B-29. *Bock's Car* was still at 2,000 feet and closing on the runway when the burst of fireworks startled the field into action. Traffic scattered to clear the way, but there was no time for a regular low-and-slow approach. "We'll go right down," Sweeney said to the copilot, Captain Charles Albury. "Tell them to brace for a rough one." *Bock's Car* came in fast and high, hit halfway down the runway and, as the port outboard engine quit, yawed toward a row of parked planes. Sweeney regained control, hit the brakes and stopped the plane on the last 10 feet of runway.

Out of curiosity, Kuharek later drained and measured the fuel remaining in the tanks. It came to seven gallons.

EYEWITNESS TO DOOMSDAY

SCENES OF HORROR THAT SEARED THE SOUL

A tattered child flees the Hiroshima holocaust. The image still haunted 74-year-old Sadako Kimura when she drew this scene nearly 30 years later.

Pika-don was the name the Japanese invented to describe the unimaginably powerful weapons that exploded over Hiroshima on August 6, 1945, and over Nagasaki three days later. The term combines the word for "lightning flash" with the sound of an explosion; its syllables faintly imitate a sky-splitting crackle followed by a thunderclap. What happened next remained stamped forever in the minds of those who witnessed the calamity and lived to tell about it.

There were almost no survivors within a 500-yard radius of Ground Zero, the point above which the bombs exploded. Those beyond that lethal range recalled seeing in the first seconds a brilliant blue-white flash that became a burgeoning orange ball, emitting unbearable heat. Almost at once a violent blast of air shredded buildings, clothes and flesh, and everything combustible seemed to take fire.

The appalling hours that followed are illustrated on these pages by eyewitnesses who almost 30 years later were inspired by a Japanese television documentary to turn to art as a forum for recording—and exorcising—their memories of the awful event. Using pencils, crayons, paints or marking pens, more than 1,000 ordinary citizens of Hiroshima and Nagasaki called upon their nightmarish recollections to create images that are more vivid than any professional could have produced. The Japan Broadcasting Corporation assembled the drawings for public exhibition, and selections were later featured in a book entitled *Unforgettable Fire*.

The artists felt compelled to pass on their memories to a generation they fervently hoped would thereby sense the horror of war without experiencing it at first hand. "I still cannot erase the scene from my memory," said one aged survivor. "Before I died, I had to draw it and leave it for others." Some intended their art as a visual prayer, adding the character symbolizing folded hands as an expression of the sorrow of the living for the dead. And more than a few were frustrated by the impossibility of fully conveying what they remembered. One elderly woman made sketch after sketch, then exclaimed bitterly: "Even if I drew a hundred pictures, they could not tell you of my experiences."

From Mount Futaba, a mile and a half from the Hiroshima blast center, Goro Kiyoyoshi watched the Shukkeien Garden (center) burst into flame as a mushroom cloud rose over the city. On the near shore of the Ota River, people he depicted as white stick-figures flee from the blast.

二葉山から見た　第二総軍と饒津神社
夢の元安城と鶴目黄金をはさんで市内全所は
火の海と戠った原爆の木の子雲と太田川

比治山本町□月八
喜代吉
五郎

REMEMBERING THOSE WHO COULD NOT ESCAPE

About 10 minutes after the bomb struck Hiroshima, a woman trapped in the wreckage of a burning house cries for help. The sound of her voice tortured the memory of Kanichi Ito, who was unable to assist her. Helplessness in the face of suffering was a recurrent theme.

Pinned with her infant beneath the beams of a collapsed and smoking roof, a mother calls 'Someone, please help this child!' Hatsuji Takeuchi, at the age of 58, drew this picture with colored pencils in remembrance of two lives that he was unable to save.

Pleading for help, two terribly burned victims lie outside the Hiroshima railway station, in this painting by Shouichi Furukawa. Many who survived the initial blast died painfully from burns caused by the bomb's thermal wave or by the conflagration that raged for two days afterward.

昭和二十年八月七日午前

広島駅前派出所と隣り左り

駅前郵便局（と思いますが）の間で

下裁きになった女の人が助け

をよんでいた石段のところに男の人

が中には人らしきものが……火が

もえていた……

''Is this the end of my life?'' thought Yoshiko Michitsuji, who, at the age of 48, painted this watercolor picture of herself and another girl dashing barefoot and bleeding ''through a sea of fire that was barely passable.''

山本芳子

陽炎

場所 天満町電車通り

人々は、水を求めて、防火

用水にむらがった。

水を飲むと、そのまゝ、

ガックリと息絶えた

槽内に浮んでいた

年若い掃除の死体

赤絵具を塗るに

胸が痛む

Victims of burns, blast and radiation, one of
them a pregnant woman, expire at a water tank
where they sought to slake the raging thirst
experienced by all those who were exposed to
the explosion. Hiroshima resident Akira
Onoki was 16 when he witnessed this scene.

On the steps of a monument, Kazuo
Matsumuro (right) lies crippled and bleeding.
The face of the man next to him was
so badly burned that Matsumuro did not at

Three young women hobble toward Hiroshima Public Hospital, their arms extended to keep the burned and peeling flesh from rubbing against their bodies. In her inscription, artist Asa Shigemori wrote that fright had caused the women's hair to stand on end.

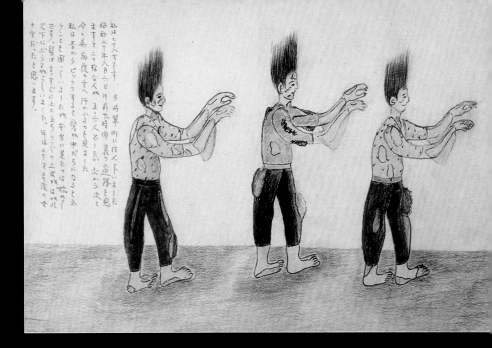

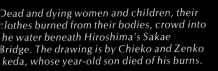

Dead and dying women and children, their clothes burned from their bodies, crowd into the water beneath Hiroshima's Sakae Bridge. The drawing is by Chieko and Zenko Ikeda, whose year-old son died of his burns.

①

昭和二十年八月六日午前九時頃

市内新庄橋附近

広島市皆実町17丁目 10-22
小林正男 75歳
TEL 51-4802

Forty-five minutes after the blast, refugees cross the Shinjo Bridge just outside Hiroshima, their limbs held in positions characteristic of massive-burn victims. Masao Kobayashi drew this vividly remembered scene at 75.

Seeking water, Kinzo Nishida brings his badly injured wife to a riverbank. He recalls with horror seeing ''a stark-naked man who was standing in the rain holding one of his eyeballs in the palm of his hand.''

Ash-blackened radioactive rain falls on a group of scorched-naked schoolgirls and two straggling boys (right) following a teacher seeking shelter. In artist Kishiro Nagara's inscription, one of the two children sprawled at left pleads, ''Don't die, brother!''

THE GHASTLY WEAPON'S GROTESQUE EFFECTS

The dead hand "was lifted to the sky and the fingers were burning with blue flames," wrote Akiko Takakura, who was then 18 years old, of the strange incandescence that afflicted many of the Hiroshima victims.

In the gutted remains of a trolley car, the woman operator lies dead. "How strange," marveled the artist, Junjiro Wataoka. "Her black hair was perfectly straight."

Near a water tank piled with corpses stands "the petrified body of a woman, with one leg lifted as though running, her baby tightly clutched in her arms," recalled Yasuko Yamagata, who was 17 in 1945. "The memory," she said, "will never leave me."

The body of a little girl is huddled against the stone embankment of the Enko River, where she died nursing her wounds. Masato Yamashita remembered finding her there three days after the Hiroshima bombing

猿猴川におりて、たすける人の
ないまま、息絶えた娘
8月9日
え 山下正人

njured refugees in Nagasaki clamber aboard a train about two miles
from the center of destruction, in this painting by Kunito Terai, a 19-year-
old engineer on one of the trains that shuttled victims out of the city.
Another rescuer recalled that "almost all of them died soon after."

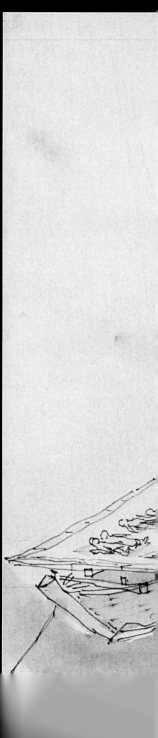

SUCCOR FOR THE SURVIVORS

Tended by soldiers, the wounded from Hiroshima's Kanawa Island are towed on hastily contrived rafts to Otake Marine Corps Base, an eight-hour voyage. "We could do nothing for the injured people but give them water," wrote Yoshimi Hara, who drew this picture at the age of 55. "There was only one medical orderly for each string of five rafts."

数日後、金輪島より大竹海兵団に
被爆者を運ぶ。
引船一隻に団のような門橋、五隻、
一隻の門橋に下士官二名、兵三名、救援
の竹添、約三名、被爆者、辛一名、
水と手えらの粕一杯なり。止血帯
かけはずれて動脈から大勢の血の所、
鳩さん、口を動かせ数がスイカを割
在様なら人、こんな毎五隻に看
護兵一名なのだ
朝五時に出航午炊一は大竹着た
その時、敵機来襲、機関砲撃を受
し、何の術も無く毛布をかけるのみ
その門、五十名中二名、死亡二名は二
荊町の五十年甦二万勇さの名名と叫び起
あがり、散兵はつくりと思えた。後だったな
こくらか鬼さんは他隊え収容されてしたな
兄と闖た、一名は手板のついた娘さんる
つら、

Ranks of the injured stretch as far as the eye can see in Kiyoshi Wakai's watercolor painting of a makeshift aid station on a Hiroshima riverbank. Relief workers pass out rice balls and water as fires burn nearby in what one survivor called ''an inferno of heat, sickness and death.''

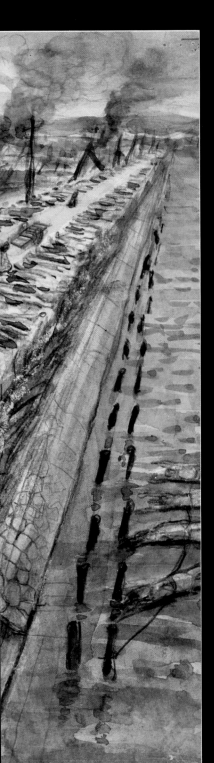

"There was not enough room for the injured in the Red Cross hospital," recalled Tomiko Ikeshoji, who was a teenager in Hiroshima in 1945. "They lay at the entrance, asking for water, water."

In Kizo Kawakami's vivid recollection of an outdoor aid station in Hiroshima, a mother, with dressings on her burns, nurses her child while an attendant peels charred clothing from a woman's wounds.

FIRES OF GRIEF FOR THE DEAD

A family prays at the funeral pyre of two
sisters in a painting by Hiroshi Matsuzoe, who
at 14 was about the same age as the victims.
He remembered that their faces ''were made up
beautifully,'' and they were dressed in
kimonos usually worn on festive occasions.

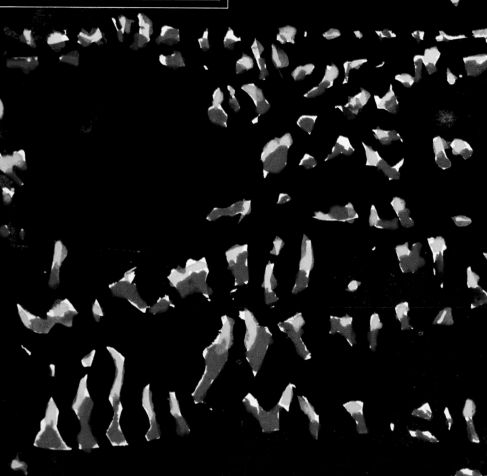

Looking from a hilltop across devastated
Nagasaki, Yoshito Nagamatsu recalled, ''All
one can see are fires, fires, fires—funeral
pyres burning under the night sky of August.''

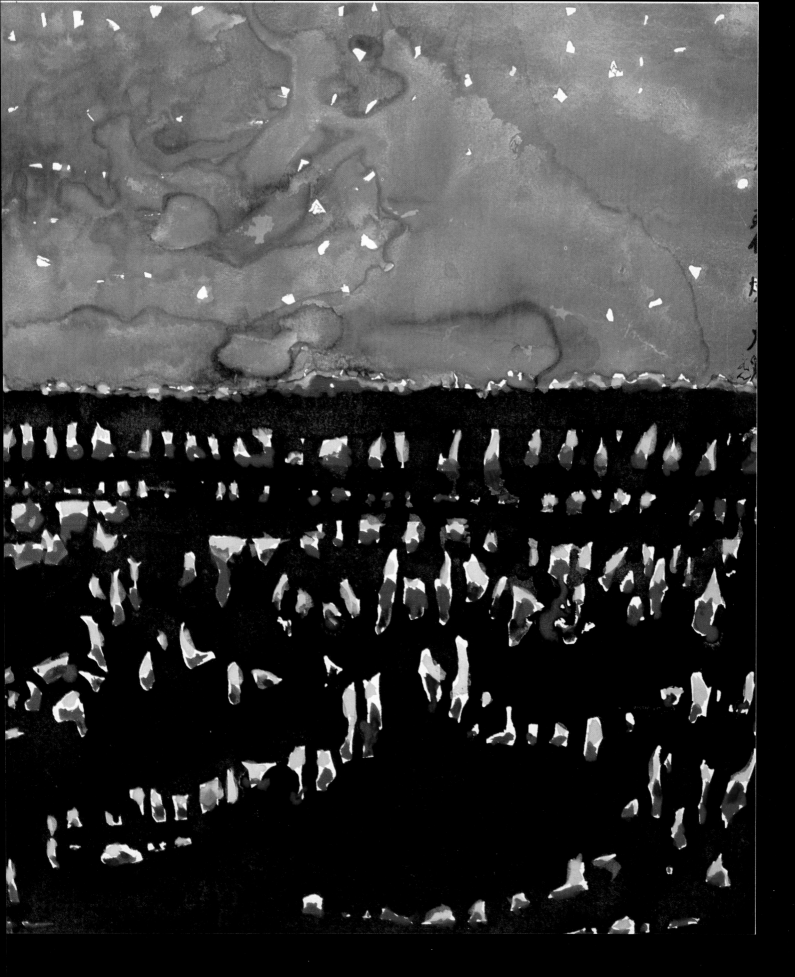

119

4

August 6 had dawned clear and hot over Hiroshima. By 8 a.m. the city's 245,000 civilian residents, weary after two false air-raid alerts during the night and another that morning, were settling into the routine of a wartime day. The city on the southwestern coast of Honshu had never been severely bombed by the B-san (Mister B, as the B-29s were called), and the longer Hiroshima was spared the more apprehensive the people became; they worried that they were being saved for a special punishment.

At Hiroshima's West Parade Ground a group of Army inductees, men over 40, had just said their sad farewells to wives and children. Soldiers crowded the barracks of the 11th Infantry Regiment and others performed calisthenics in the courtyard of the Chugoku Military District Headquarters. In nearby Hiroshima Castle, where the crews of two B-29s shot down a few days earlier were being held, the 23 captive Americans had already finished eating their morning meal of mush.

Elsewhere in and around Hiroshima, the day had begun for a number of others who were destined to play special roles in the tragic drama about to unfold. In the western suburb of Koi, the Reverend Kiyoshi Tanimoto, a Methodist minister who had studied in Atlanta, Georgia, was helping a friend unload a handcart full of household goods they had brought from the city for safekeeping. Near the center of Hiroshima, Dr. Michihiko Hachiya, medical director of the hospital attached to the government's Communications Bureau (postal, telephone and telegraph center), sprawled on the straw-mat covering of his living-room floor; as the hospital's air-raid warden he had been up all night, and he was exhausted. Not far away, Shigeyoshi Morimoto, a kite maker by trade, shopped in a supply store for paintbrushes. Morimoto's home was in the city of Nagasaki, but for several months he had been employed in Hiroshima, making anti-aircraft kites for the Army. Eight miles west of the city, Satoshi Nakamura, a reporter for the Domei News Agency, was just sitting down to breakfast in the home of a friend.

At 8:16 a.m., an unimaginable incandescence swallowed the sky and outshone the sun. A gigantic hemisphere of superheated air, so compressed that it became visible, formed and rushed outward in every direction at 1,200 feet per second. Wooden buildings within two miles of the explosion burst instantly into flames. The heat in the fireball cre-

SOME WHO SURVIVED

ated above the city was later calculated to have reached 540,000° F. The hypocenter, or Ground Zero—a point directly below the fireball about 300 yards from the Aioi Bridge—was blasted by 11,000° F. heat and air pressure that reached eight tons per square yard. The Shima Clinic, a private hospital located at Ground Zero, was virtually vaporized. All that was left upright were the concrete pillars at the clinic entrance, and the pressure from above had driven them straight down into the ground. Within 1,000 yards of Ground Zero, the surface of granite building stones melted. At 600 yards, clay roof tiles with a melting point of 2,300° F. dissolved, and mica fused on the surfaces of gravestones.

Of those who survived anywhere near the center of the blast—and they were few—almost no one could afterward remember hearing an explosion. Farther away, the sound of the detonation was monstrous; in the seaport of Kure, 12 miles distant, people thought a nearby ammunition dump had blown up. In a house eight miles away, the reporter Nakamura was thrown to the floor and all the windows of the house facing east toward Hiroshima splintered into fragments. Scrambling to his feet, Nakamura rushed outside. He saw a thick pillar of black smoke rushing upward out of the heart of the city; at what he estimated to be 15,000 feet or more, the pillar burst into a boiling globe of red flame, like the sudden blooming of a grotesque flower. Nakamura rushed for his bicycle and pedaled toward the low-hanging black and yellow cloud that now shrouded what was left of the city.

The Reverend Tanimoto, unloading the cart in the driveway of a friend's home, was aware of the enormous flash nearly two miles away and flung himself between two boulders. He heard nothing, but seconds later he felt a wave of air pressure and he huddled closer to the rocks as debris rained down on him. Tanimoto got to his feet and saw that the house was gone, smashed flat. Leaving his friend behind, he ran to the roadway and saw a gang of soldiers who had been digging a bomb shelter. They were coming out of the pit and he saw that they were bleeding.

The minister ran toward the smoking city, desperately anxious about his church and his parishioners. He was equally concerned about his wife and infant son; as a precaution he sent them every night to Ushida, a distant suburb, but they were due back by now.

Although Morimoto the kite maker was relatively close to the hypocenter, he was miraculously shielded by the walls of the paint store in which he was shopping. In a daze he made his way into the open and through the burning city. Barely aware of time or distance, he eventually found his way to a railroad terminus that was still operating and hitched a ride on a coal car, intending to return home to his wife in Nagasaki.

Dr. Hachiya, who was resting in his living room, was startled by sudden, intense flashes of light. "So well does one recall little things," he wrote later in his diary, "that I remember vividly how a stone lantern in the garden became brilliantly lighted. Garden shadows disappeared. The view where, a moment before, all had been so bright and sunny, was now dark and hazy. Through swirling dust I could barely discern a wooden column that had supported one corner of my house. It was leaning crazily and the roof sagged." At that point, wrote the physician, "I discovered to my surprise that I was completely naked. How odd!"

Through fallen beams, Hachiya made his way into the garden. Taking stock of himself, he found that the entire right side of his body was cut and bleeding. A huge splinter protruded from a wound in his thigh. Blood began to spurt from his face and, feeling with his hand, he discovered that his lower lip was terribly gashed. He also found a large fragment of glass embedded in his neck. He pulled the glass free and then began to worry that it had severed the carotid artery and he would bleed to death.

Dr. Hachiya remembered his wife and began to shout for her, "Yaeko! Yaeko!" She emerged from the wreckage holding one elbow, her clothing torn and bloodied and her eyebrows burned away. The house was falling around them and he told her they had to flee. The best path to the street seemed to lead through the remains of the house next door. Going through the gate to the street, the doctor tripped. He saw that he had stumbled over a dead man's head.

"I'm sorry! I'm sorry, please!" he cried, on the edge of hysteria. As the couple stood in the street, their house collapsed in a heap. Then, as other houses fell and began to burn, they started for the hospital. For Hachiya, now wearing his wife's apron to cover his nakedness, it was slow going through the littered streets, with an inferno of burning houses erupting on both sides. Hachiya suddenly felt an overpowering thirst. It was the most common early symptom experienced by the survivors of the atomic bomb. An overwhelming weakness came upon him and he told his wife to go ahead without him.

Gradually some strength returned. Dr. Hachiya stumbled on through the murk of dust and smoke. He became aware of other staggering figures in the gloom. Many walked stiffly, holding their arms out from their bodies, hands and forearms dangling. Dully he recognized that they had been burned; their strange posture prevented one burned surface from rubbing painfully against another. He saw a naked woman with a naked baby in her arms; he averted his eyes, wishing not to embarrass her. He was struck by the uncanny silence; nobody spoke, moaned, wept or screamed; they moved like ghosts.

Hachiya reached the hospital—a concrete structure still largely intact—and collapsed on a stretcher. He was soon brought abruptly out of his semiconscious state by frightful pain as a nurse began to paint his torn chest with iodine. He realized for the first time that the hospital and the building next to it were engulfed by flames, every window space revealing a wall of fire. He was carried into the hospital garden, dimly aware that other patients were being helped out of the building. He lay on his stretcher, staring upward while the flames bred violent drafts that sent sheets of zinc roofing soaring aloft in whirling, dizzying flight. Chunks of flaming wood arced upward and fell; one hot ember landed on his ankle. Amid the chaos, he recognized his wife, who had also reached the hospital.

That night the hospital's chief surgeon sewed up Hachiya's torn face and thigh and some 30 other cuts and gashes on his body. When the fires died and the hospital cooled enough, the staff and their increasing horde of patients moved back into the shell of the building; at least it provided some shelter. Hachiya, though gravely wounded, would soon contribute importantly to the recuperation of Hiroshima's survivors.

Slowly, by agonizing degrees, a grotesque sort of life began to stir beneath the shroud of smoke and yellow dust that had been Hiroshima. The Reverend Tanimoto, who was uninjured and running toward the city, started to meet people coming out of the ruins. They moved like automatons, marching blindly around and over fallen telephone poles, tangles of wire and other debris, their eyes downcast or straight ahead, not speaking.

Tanimoto was struck by how many of the people were stark-naked. The heat of the bomb had burned most of the clothing from their bodies, and the blast that followed had ripped away the remaining tatters. Those who were wearing dark clothing, which absorbed heat, were the most horribly burned. Those in white or light colors were more fortunate; the flash reflected off white and tended not to burn. Most women in wartime Japan wore the practical *monpe*, plain or patterned baggy trousers, but a few still affected the intri-

In a damaged photo taken by a resident of Koyagi Island, clouds of smoke from the atomic bomb obscure Hiroshima, five miles away. The clouds took a unique mushroom shape and rose more than 40,000 feet.

cately figured kimono of old. It was easy to distinguish the wearers of patterned clothing from the others, for the shapes of the dark flowers on their clothes were burned into their flesh. Tanimoto felt enormous guilt at being healthy in the presence of such misery and he frequently murmured, ''Excuse me for having no burden like yours.''

As the minister ran toward his home neighborhood, he often heard the cry, ''*Tasukete kure!*'' (''Help, if you please!'') coming from under the wreckage of smashed and smoldering houses. He ran on, knowing there was no help he could give, praying as he went, ''God help them and take them out of the fire.''

Tanimoto took many detours to avoid impenetrable barriers of debris or solid walls of flame. He had run about seven miles—while trying to cover two—when the fires forced him into the swift-running Ota River. Exhausted, he nearly drowned before staggering up on the opposite bank. He ran again, and near a still-standing Shinto shrine he met a woman carrying an infant. He nearly passed her before he realized that she was his wife. Physically and emotionally spent, he could only say, ''Oh, you are safe.'' She had returned from Ushida early that morning. The air pressure had collapsed the parsonage on top of her and the baby, and it had taken her half an hour to dig the baby and herself out of

A cluster of stunned and exhausted survivors try to find shelter on the still-intact Miyuki Bridge as flames and smoke rise from the center of Hiroshima about three hours after the explosion of the bomb.

123

the ruins. Now she was on the way back to Ushida. Tanimoto said he must see to his parishioners. They parted as undemonstratively as they had met, too shocked and worn out to say or do more.

On the East Parade Ground, which had been designated an air-raid evacuation center, Tanimoto found a scene of massive human wretchedness. The burned were moaning, *"Mizu, mizu"* ("Water, water"). In the wreckage the minister located a basin and a water tap that still worked and began carrying water, pouring it into blistered mouths. On some victims, the skin of their backs hung down like flapping shirttails.

Still searching for his parishioners, Tanimoto then made his way to Asano Sentei Park, a haven of cool greenery far enough from Ground Zero to have survived the bomb blast. Hundreds of wounded had gone to the park to escape the fires, but not long after Tanimoto arrived, flames began licking at their place of refuge. The wounded pushed down to the bank of the Kyobashi River, which bordered the park, to get away from the flames. The press of the crowd nudged many people into the river, where they drowned; the shallows became clogged with bodies.

Tanimoto looked around the riverbank for a boat. At length he came upon a heavy flat-bottomed boat surrounded by five badly burned corpses, men who evidently had died at the same instant while launching the boat. Aghast at the prospect of disturbing the dead, Tanimoto nevertheless lifted the bodies away from the craft, muttering as he did so, "Please forgive me for taking this boat. I must use it for others who are alive." He wrestled the boat into the water and, with only a bamboo pole for propulsion, began ferrying the wounded, 10 or 12 at a time, upstream to safety.

As Tanimoto continued his rescue work, a party of four men—government functionaries—arrived at the park and pressed into the solid mass of desperate humanity, heading toward the river. They were shouting "The Emperor's picture! The Emperor's picture!" One was in the lead, two served as flank guards and the fourth bore on his bent back a portrait of Hirohito in a heavy frame. The men had rescued the portrait from the endangered Communications Bureau and were taking it away from the rapidly approaching fires. The throngs of maimed, bleeding, burned and naked in the park drew back and made a pathway to the water. Soldiers drew themselves to attention and saluted the picture; civilians who were able to stand bowed in reverence and those who could not stand put their raw hands together in prayer. An officer on the bank drew his sword and bellowed at some passing boatmen. A boat made its way among the corpses to the shore and bore the portrait away to a safer place.

Late in the day, while the fires still burned, Tanimoto came upon a score of wounded too weak to move and huddled so close to the water's edge that they were sure to be engulfed by the incoming tide. He set about getting them to higher ground. They were burn victims and now, hours after the blast, their raw flesh was exuding a yellow fluid. And they stank. One by one, he lifted the soft, wet, living flesh, nerving himself to the repulsive task by repeating under his breath, "These are human beings."

But the Reverend Tanimoto's effort was in vain. When he returned the following morning, the tide had risen to cover the resting place of the people he had moved. The bodies of a few of them floated nearby.

About sundown on the day of the bombing, Tanimoto happened on a woman from his neighborhood, 20-year-old Mrs. Kamai. She was huddled on the ground, cradling her

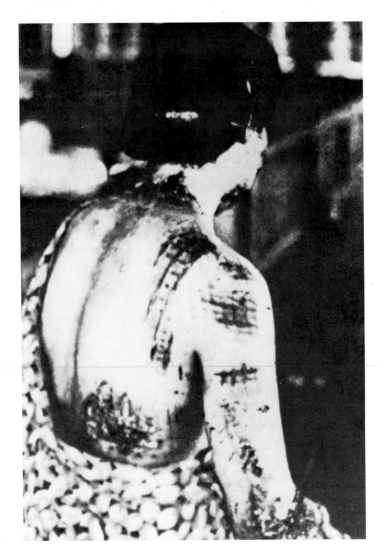

A woman exposed to the thermal rays of the atomic bomb at Hiroshima bears the imprint of the cloth pattern she was wearing. The dark, heat-absorbing designs on traditional kimonos were often burned into the skin.

A horribly burned student, her facial features all but obliterated by the heat of the bomb, lies on her back on a straw mat at the Hiroshima Red Cross Hospital. She succumbed to her wounds after four days.

infant daughter in her arms. The baby was dead. Recognizing the minister, the young woman got to her feet and asked him to find her husband. Tanimoto knew that Kamai had been inducted the day before; he had been at the Chugoku Headquarters and was therefore almost certainly wounded or dead. "I'll try," he said, thinking the woman in no condition to accept the truth.

"You must find him," she insisted. "He loved our baby so much. I want him to see her once more." For the next four days, Mrs. Kamai cuddled the small corpse and whenever Tanimoto was near he could feel her beseeching eyes on him. Finally he resorted to avoiding her deliberately; the demanding stare was more than he could bear.

The harrowing scenes of suffering witnessed by the Reverend Tanimoto and Dr. Hachiya were repeated throughout the destroyed city. The bomb had left thousands of victims to die slow, agonizing deaths. For thousands more, it had been more merciful; they had died in the blinking of an eye, so quickly that perhaps they had been unaware of dying.

A train pulling into town about a mile from Ground Zero had in an instant become a twisted, glassless, derailed skeleton. All of the passengers were dead, some in their seats, others clinging with blackened hands to the overhead support straps. Work gangs of high-school students, caught in the open, died with their tools in their hands. At Chugoku

Military District Headquarters the courtyard was piled deep with dead soldiers, scarcely recognizable as human. On one of the city's many bridges a man on his bicycle leaned upright against the guardrail, frozen in death. Out of the 11th Infantry Regiment barracks had stumbled a file of survivors, their heads swollen to great glistening mounds of flesh, ears gone, eyes gone, noses gone. One with no lips croaked his need for water.

At the Hiroshima Prefectural Daiichi Middle School, about 1,000 yards from Ground Zero, 150 teenagers had been outside the building; all were obliterated in their tracks. Of another 150 inside the school, 133 were killed at once or died before the day was over. Survivors ran for a nearby swimming pool to escape the heat of the burning building. Soon the pool was full of dead bodies, some killed by burns and others by drowning because they were too weak to stay afloat.

At the gate of the West Parade Ground, the overage inductees and their well-wishers lay dead in family groups. None of the 23 American prisoners in Hiroshima Castle survived the bomb, though three of them may have lived a little while. Witnesses described one of them, clad only in red and white underwear, dying beneath a bridge. Two more, with hands bound behind them, were reported stoned to death near one of the bridges.

Hachiroyasutaka Atago, a student, told of seeing flaming

houses toppling one after another like rows of dominoes. "Fire seemed to be rampaging through the whole city," he reported. "One boy, seared by the heat, lay on the ground, his eyes open, his hands and feet twitching. Another, also lying on the ground, was simply staring up at the sky. I spoke to him, but he made no reply. Nearby, a young man, his body terribly burned, was rolling on the scorched earth. 'Kill me!' he kept screaming. 'Will somebody please kill me?' Off to one side in a ditch floated a great number of bodies. I saw that at least one person in the ditch was still alive. He was trying to climb out. I grabbed hold of his wrists in an attempt to help him, but the skin just peeled off in my hands."

The blast that followed the flash splintered nearly every window and mirror in Hiroshima and its environs; thousands of people were wounded by the shards. Captain Goichi Sashida, who commanded an Army medical unit at an emergency-aid station, worked on the glass victims and could hear the splinters crunch together inside the flesh as he sought to extract them with a forceps. He was both astonished and moved that no one moaned or cried out during what had to be an excruciating ordeal. In Dr. Hachiya's Communications Bureau hospital a dying woman suckled her baby at a breast riddled with glass.

The bomb's unearthly phenomena did not stop with the flash and the horrendous blast, or with the fires and freak whirlwinds that followed. At various times over different areas of the ruined city, the hot air in the bomb's cloud column condensed and rain fell—a rain such as no one had seen before. The drops were huge, each as large as a man's fingertip. What was even stranger, the drops were black and they left on unburned skin gray stains that would not wash off. Those upon whom the rain fell had no way of knowing that they were being pelted by drops polluted with lethal radioactivity that had risen in the mushroom cloud.

The bomb blast and its virulent aftermath severed communications between Hiroshima and the outside world. Some time passed before the rest of Japan became aware of the seriousness of the city's nightmare. One of the first bearers of the news was Second Lieutenant Matsuo Yasuzawa, an Army pilot who was inside Hiroshima airport's control center, two miles from Ground Zero, when the bomb went off. Along with others, Yasuzawa quickly dug himself free of the wrecked building and, for a moment, stared at the damage in disbelief. Then, looking at the sky, he saw the three B-29s, mere silvery specks flying at about 30,000 feet. Yasuzawa was overcome with rage. He began to run down the flight line, dodging around burning planes and fuel trucks, to the aircraft he had landed in less than an hour earlier, after a flight from his base at Shimonoseki, 100 miles away. Even though the Ki-55 Advance Trainer would stand little chance against a Superfortress, Yasuzawa wanted revenge.

When he reached his plane, Yasuzawa found that its metal frame, having been broadside to the blast, was now bent into an arc and resembled a banana. The young pilot was not deterred. He climbed aboard and punched the starter button; the plane's engine kicked over, coughed and started. At that point Yasuzawa looked up from the controls and saw a sight that made him cringe: The first wave of walking wounded emerged from the dust cloud onto the airfield, seeking refuge from the spreading fires. Bleeding, naked, charred, trailing strips of skin, they walked in such profound shock that they seemed in a trance, oblivious to their terrible wounds and the roaring of Yasuzawa's engine.

Seeing this unearthly procession, Yasuzawa was seized by a new urgency—to get away and report that something

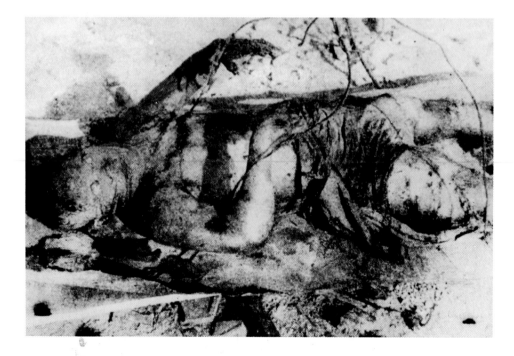

The rigid corpse of a person who was charred by the thermal wave of the atomic bomb lies on a parade ground in Hiroshima about 800 yards from the hypocenter.

terrible had happened to Hiroshima. He gunned the engine and the plane skittered crab-fashion down the runway. When it reached flying speed, he eased back on the stick. Incredibly, the twisted aircraft lifted into the air and flew. Leaning to his left to get protection from what remained of the shattered windshield, Yasuzawa began to climb, struggling with controls that barely functioned. Around 2,000 feet he leveled off and circled the city for five minutes, unaware that he was flying in and out of a radioactive cloud. Then he put the crooked plane on a wobbly course for his home base to report what he had seen: that Hiroshima no longer existed.

A similar urgency galvanized Satoshi Nakamura, the Domei News Agency reporter who had witnessed the bomb's detonation from a suburban house. After exploring to the edge of the city and witnessing the ghastly parade of survivors trudging mindlessly out of the ruins, he made his way to the Japan Broadcasting Corporation's station some three miles from Ground Zero. Though its transmitting equipment was a shambles, the station did possess the one remaining usable telephone line anywhere near Hiroshima. The line ran to Okayama, 90 miles away. Nakamura used it to dictate a bulletin for relay to the Domei bureau in Tokyo: "At around 8:16 a.m., August 6, one or two enemy planes flew over Hiroshima and dropped one or two special bombs (they may have been atomic), completely destroying the city. Casualties are estimated at 170,000 dead."

Later in the afternoon, having prepared a more detailed report, Nakamura got through again, this time to a Domei editor in Okayama. To his dismay, the reporter heard himself berated instead of praised for his initiative. The editor accused him of exaggeration; the report that one or two bombs could wipe out a city and kill 170,000 people was ridiculous. He urged Nakamura to curb his imagination in his forthcoming longer file. He started to say, "Why, the Army itself . . .," but he got no further because Nakamura, scenes of catastrophe fresh in his mind, exploded with rage.

"You tell those bastards in the Army that they are the world's biggest fools," he yelled. "I'll give you a second story and I'll give it to you now. Just tell those bastards in the Army to read it!"

The reporter then dictated from his notebook a detailed account of the horrors he had witnessed that day: the mass exodus of the half-alive victims and the grisly nature of their wounds. He told of seeing windrows of charred bodies and of smelling burning flesh. Nakamura gave his story in the measured tones of a professional journalist, oblivious to the tears that coursed down his cheeks and fell on the notebook from which he read.

For the tens of thousands who were wounded on the day of the blast, no proper medical care existed. Finding first aid was nearly impossible. Fifty-two of the city's 55 hospitals and aid centers were destroyed or severely damaged. Of 150 doctors practicing in Hiroshima, 65 were killed and most of the others were wounded in varying degrees. Of 1,780 nurses, 1,654 died or were injured. At the new Red Cross Hospital, only six physicians and 10 nurses were healthy enough to work. The few doctors left in the city, moreover, had pathetically little equipment or medicine on hand. Such items had long been scarce on the home front. As the War widened and shortages squeezed the nation, the armed forces had commandeered a lion's share of Japan's medical supplies. Now the bomb had destroyed most of the available instruments, dressings and medicines.

Here and there, searches among the debris of a demolished clinic or hospital turned up a few dressings, some intact containers of Mercurochrome or iodine, and a few pre-

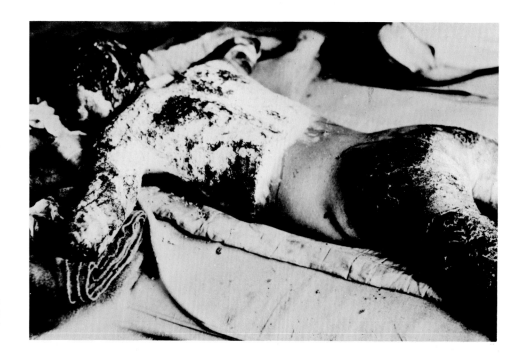

His festering arms propped up by blankets, a man suffering fatal burns passes the last hours of his life face down on a cot in an Army quarantine station near Hiroshima.

cious instruments—but almost no anesthetics. Even the worst burn cases got only rudimentary treatment: dressings soaked in a saline solution or applications of a zinc powder suspended in vegetable oil. It was a day for dying.

In midmorning of August 9, the freight train carrying Shigeyoshi Morimoto, the kite maker fleeing home from the nightmare of Hiroshima three days earlier, reached its terminus in Nagasaki. Morimoto jumped down and hurried off toward his shop near the city's center. He was a driven man, profoundly shaken by his experience, deeply worried about the safety of his own family and his city. By 11:02 a.m. he had reached home and was just beginning to blurt out the terrifying story to his wife. "A great blue flash . . ." he began to say, when the light came again, stupefying in its intensity. Morimoto dropped to his knees, ripped open the trap door to the cellar, shoved his wife and infant son into the hole and dropped in after them. All around them the earth shuddered, but the Morimotos were safe.

The family had been saved entirely by chance. Thirty thousand feet above Nagasaki, bombardier Kermit Beahan had been forced by cloud cover to choose an alternate aiming point for his plutonium bomb. Had the drop gone as planned, the bomb would have descended almost directly on Morimoto's shop, in the heart of Nagasaki's commercial district. Instead it detonated about two miles away, and Morimoto lived through two atomic attacks.

The city of Nagasaki lay in two valleys, separated by a mountainous ridge that sloped down to the East China Sea. One valley embraced the old section of the city and the commercial center. The longer valley, called Urakami for its river, contained most of Nagasaki's manufacturing and heavy industry. In those two valleys, 200,000 people lived and worked. When the bomb fell off target, much of the Old City was spared. The bomb exploded 1,500 feet above the Urakami valley, over the city's ripest military targets: the Mitsubishi complex of steel and arms factories. The war plants were smashed along with nearly everything else up and down the valley.

The physical destruction was a virtual carbon copy of the ruin of Hiroshima. Under the boiling mushroom cloud raged fires that consumed dwellings and shops by the thousands. Whirlwinds whipped the debris aloft into dizzying flight and the deadly black rain descended. At the mouth of the Urakami River, spherical gas tanks became gigantic fireballs that flew into the sky, sank back to earth, then soared skyward again.

Out of the turbulent gloom marched a stumbling, stunned parade of thousands: the naked, the blackened, the glass-riddled, the faceless.

Here and there an individual escaped. At Saint Francis Convent, 15 nuns and students that morning were scattering fertilizer in a field. When they heard the sound of aircraft approaching, 14 of them dropped their tools and fled toward a riverbank they hoped would afford protection. The eldest, 64-year-old Sister Noguchi, who was in charge of

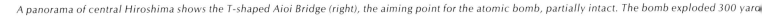

A panorama of central Hiroshima shows the T-shaped Aioi Bridge (right), the aiming point for the atomic bomb, partially intact. The bomb exploded 300 yard

the party, kept working until the fertilizer was gone. Then she ran, in a direction opposite from the rest; she soon tripped and fell into an eight-foot ditch. At that moment the great flash ignited the sky and the heat and blast enveloped the convent and the fields. When Sister Noguchi crawled out into the burning desolation, untouched, she found all her companions dead.

On the grounds of the Yamazato Primary School, about 1,000 yards from Ground Zero, Mrs. Tae Adachi, a teacher, had been working with others of the staff in a garden. Shortly before 11 a.m. she went alone to the school building for a cup of tea. She had kicked off her shoes and was beginning to relax when the bomb's glare turned everything white and she was thrown to the floor. As she lost consciousness, she saw a wall across the room slowly collapse, and she was showered with plaster and tiles.

When Mrs. Adachi came to, the shattered room was full of her colleagues who had been outside when the bomb struck. Now they were partially naked, and their bared breasts and buttocks reminded her of red pomegranates. After helping to tend the wounded at the school, she set out for her home. She had not seen her three children since early morning. When she reached the place where her house should have been, she found it gone; nothing remained in the hot ashes but one of her children's lunch boxes. Impulsively she moved forward, and searing pain shot up her legs; only then did she realize she was barefoot.

Mrs. Adachi hunkered beside the desolate ruin until near-ly dark, then wandered back toward the schoolhouse—now in flames. In a bomb shelter near the school, she came upon her children, all unhurt, watching the school burn. They had been horrified at the thought that their mother must be in the burning building. A chance decision had saved the children's lives. Just before the explosion, they had gone into the bomb shelter to get the sleeping mats that they absent-mindedly had left there that morning.

Fate had toyed with the living elsewhere in Nagasaki. On the roof of the five-story electric company building, a carpenter named Matsumoto and a companion were constructing a wooden storage bin. When they heard the distant hum of the B-29s they briefly debated retiring to a shelter, but decided against it on the grounds that the Americans seldom bombed from such a high altitude. When the flash came, both men instinctively started to run. Matsumoto's partner sprinted for the exit stairway; the blast slammed him against the concrete stairwell housing, crushing his skull. Matsumoto ran toward the building parapet; the blast lifted and flung him over the edge. He came down upright, legs still pumping, and hit the ground running, 53 feet below. He ran into the lobby of the building, where an unbelieving stare from the assistant building manager finally brought him up short. Only then did he realize what had happened, and he fainted from fright. Afterward, Matsumoto became angry when listeners refused to believe him, even though he cited the opinions of experts, who credited a freak upward air draft with gently lowering him five stories.

way, above the Shima Clinic (red dot), generating heat and shock waves that vaporized people, incinerated wood buildings and turned heavier ones to rubble.

At a pool in the Urakami River, Koichi Nakajima, aged 11, and nine of his friends were playing a swimming game they called "find the bell." Except for loincloths, they were naked. On the riverbank, Koichi flipped a small gilded bell into the water, counted to three, yelled "Here we go!" and they all dived in. The boys came up puffing, but nobody had retrieved the bell.

The failure worried Koichi. He had borrowed the bell from his sister without her knowledge, and if he could not find it, there would be trouble. Filling his lungs with air, he dived again and headed for the bottom. He surfaced less than a minute later into a world he no longer recognized. Two of his friends writhed and screamed on the bank. The other seven were blackened cadavers. Nowhere in the swirling haze could he see a building still standing.

As the mushroom cloud rose over Nagasaki, a Japanese seaplane from the nearby Navy base at Sasebo flew toward the stricken city. The three men in the aircraft—the pilot, Second Lieutenant Nobukazu Komatsu, another lieutenant named Tomimura, and a chief petty officer named Umeda—were consumed by curiosity. Two nights earlier

the men, all trainees in the Sasebo Navy Cadet Corps, had heard the American President's announcement that Hiroshima had been destroyed by an atomic bomb. At 11:05 this morning, the cadet corps had picked up a radio bulletin of a "great bombing in Nagasaki city."

Suspecting that this must be another atomic bomb—though they did not know what that was—Komatsu and his companions made an unauthorized takeoff to get a first-hand look at the phenomenon. Approaching the city at 10,000 feet, Komatsu was spellbound by the towering black cloud with its churning, expanding, malevolent dome perhaps another 15,000 feet above him.

"Let's cut into the cloud," he shouted to the others, and without waiting for an answer he banked the aircraft. Inside the cloud they were immersed in total blackness. The cabin became almost unbearably hot; Komatsu opened his window and stuck a gloved hand into the slipstream. Instantly he yanked it back; he felt as though he had been blasted with live steam. He noticed that his glove was covered with sticky gray dust.

Behind him someone screamed; Umeda was vomiting.

In search of help, a boy carrying his younger brother, whose face is caked with dried blood, wanders dazedly in the vicinity of the Nagasaki Railroad Station on the day after the explosion.

Their faces still blank from horror and shock almost 24 hours after the bomb blast, a bandaged mother and her son in Nagasaki clutch their emergency ration—balls of boiled rice distributed by a relief party.

As the heat grew more intense Tomimura opened another window, then recoiled as a blowtorch blast of air struck his face. "Close it!" Komatsu yelled. All at once they were out in sunlight again. They had been inside the lethally radioactive cloud column for eight minutes.

Komatsu landed in Nagasaki harbor and beached the plane. He and Tomimura walked into the city, leaving behind Umeda, who was too sick to move. Encountering a stumbling cavalcade of the walking dead, Tomimura broke down in tears. Later, unable to do much to help, they returned to the plane and the three men flew back to Sasebo. Their impromptu outing in the A-bomb cloud proved costly. All three men were afflicted with aftereffects of radiation poisoning. Umeda died of leukemia in 1947, Tomimura in 1964. Komatsu suffered from chronic anemia for years.

The airmen were granted a few years of extra life, but thousands of other victims in Nagasaki died of radiation sickness within days, or even hours, of the bomb blast. This brand-new and mysterious disease was all the more insid-ious because it often struck down those who otherwise had escaped the bomb's horror without a scratch. While searching for wounded in Nagasaki, the director of the city's rescue corps, a man named Toyoshima, stumbled on four apparently unhurt persons huddled in a bomb shelter: a mother, a boy about 12 years old, a girl of nine and a boy of six. Though they were not marked, the family was terrified and unwilling to venture into the grotesque world outside.

Toyoshima decided to take them on as a personal responsibility and, whenever he could spare a little time, he returned to the shelter carrying food and water. The children warmed to him and began addressing him as "Uncle Policeman." In spite of his care, however, life in the shelter was changing for the worse. On the second day, the two older children were inert and weak and Toyoshima had to cradle their heads and lift them up to dribble a little food into their mouths. On his next visit a few hours later, both were dead. And now the mother appeared listless. He tried to reassure her and gave the surviving boy a present, a

On the day after the atomic bomb was dropped on Nagasaki, a wounded woman sips water from a canteen while her moribund companions sit or sprawl lethargically amidst the ruins of the city.

wooden doll he had picked up in the wreckage outside.

The next day the small, incredibly dirty six-year-old appeared at Toyoshima's makeshift headquarters, clutching the doll in one grimy fist and a few coins in the other. "Mother died," he told Toyoshima. "Here," he said, opening the hand that held the money.

"You keep it," Toyoshima replied, and delegated a policeman to look after the boy.

The policeman did as he was bidden, using Toyoshima's own house to bathe the boy and prepare food for him. But in the process the child seemed to grow weak and began to bleed from the mouth, so the policeman took him to an emergency-aid center where he was assured the child would be cared for.

Toyoshima, learning of this, became alarmed; he walked to the rescue center to find the child. But the frantically overworked staff there could find no record of the boy, and no one appeared to remember him. Unwilling to believe that the boy had vanished without a trace, Toyoshima began questioning patients. A bandaged old man provided the answer. The boy was dead, the body already cremated. "He gave me this—a present," the old man said, and held out the scarred wooden doll.

In Hiroshima, meanwhile, dying had become the most commonplace of occurrences. People died where they fell, or they were carried or dragged themselves to some ruined clinic or hospital where most of the staff had died or were dying. At the wrecked Communications Bureau hospital, patients filled every nook of the gutted building and lay gasping on the grounds outside. To Dr. Hachiya, the hospital's medical director immobilized by his wounds, the patients smelled collectively like burning hair and excreta, which they had to deposit where they lay. He agonized over his inability to offer aid to the suffering.

"You should be thankful that you are going to live," admonished his colleague Dr. Katsube, showing no sympathy with Hachiya's impatience. "You can't get up until your sutures are out, and that won't be for at least a week."

The patients were dying so quickly that there was little time to mourn them or even to treat the bodies with traditional respect. At first the attendants shrouded the corpses in white blankets. Dr. Hachiya ordered the practice stopped, though his directive made him feel callous. Blankets were scarce, and the living needed them more than the dead.

The mounting toll of dead forced the hospital staff to improvise their own crematory, which they set up within 100 feet of the hospital. Fuel was no problem; all Hiroshima was full of combustible wreckage. The work was delegated to a man named Kitao, who had been employed in the hospital's business office. Kitao's technique was to arrange the corpses on a pyre of broken desks, packing crates or anything else that would burn. When sufficient material was available, two nurses threw on a shroud, after which Kitao placed a heavy sheet of zinc roofing over the bodies and lighted the fire. To Hachiya, it seemed that the burning bodies smelled like grilled fish.

On August 11, Hachiya's dozens of lacerations appeared sufficiently knitted and Katsube took out the stitches. Hachiya regained his feet and, though still wobbly, he immediately began making rounds. After seeing the 150 or more patients still crowded into the hospital, the doctor was per-

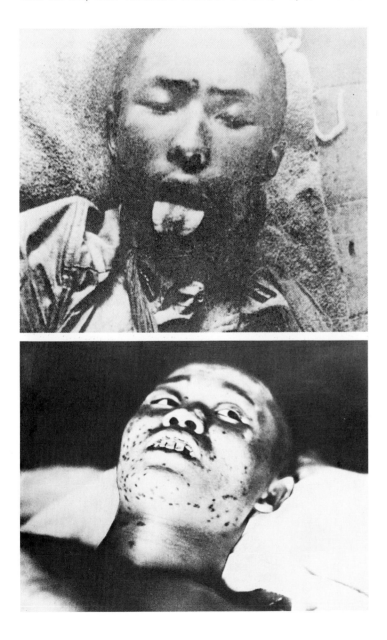

Two men dying of radiation poisoning in Hiroshima exhibit the grisly symptoms that indicate progressive deterioration of their internal organs. A laborer (top), who had been cleaning up debris after the bombing, hemorrhages from the mouth; the face of the soldier at bottom is dotted with purple spots that mark multiple hemorrhages under the skin.

plexed. The wounds of the burned, gashed and torn were obvious and terrible enough. But other patients, apparently unhurt, were developing symptoms he could not understand. Small, inexplicable hemorrhages appeared in the mouth and under the skin of one man. Many others were afflicted by severe diarrhea and could not stop coughing and vomiting blood. "Among these patients there was not one with symptoms typical of anything we knew," Hachiya wrote. "The only possible cause for the weird symptoms observed was a sudden change in atmospheric pressure. I had read somewhere about bleeding that follows ascent to high altitudes and about bleeding in deep-sea divers."

There was also a rumor, one increasingly believed by the victims, that the Americans had seeded their devilish bomb with some virulent germ or with a lingering poison gas. As more and more apparently well persons came down with unexplainable illnesses, the conviction grew that the Americans had somehow poisoned the very atmosphere and that Hiroshima was doomed to remain uninhabitable for precisely 75 years. Dr. Hachiya's scientific mind dismissed these rumors as rubbish. But still, he wondered.

Despite word of the Nagasaki bombing and despite the broadcast from the United States describing the atom bomb, few people in Hiroshima yet knew what it was that had hit them. The ruined city no longer had newspapers or radios or even electricity. Dr. Hachiya received his first solid news six days after the blast when an old friend, the former commanding officer of a battleship, came to visit him. "It is a miracle you survived," the Navy officer told him. "After all, the explosion of an atom bomb is a terrible thing."

So at last he knew what it was. But there was nothing in that bare knowledge, or in his own experience, to advise him why it was still doing such terrible things to his patients. The doctor was as baffled as ever. The shortage of everything was maddening. He needed a microscope to begin blood studies, but all the hospital's microscopes had been turned to shards of glass and metal—even one that had been kept locked in a safe. Other elemental instruments were missing; he knew the patients were running fevers, but not even one thermometer remained to tell him how high their temperatures were.

By August 19, the death rate, which had begun to subside after the first few days, was climbing again. Although some of the bad burn cases were healing, with thick, red, rubbery scar tissue replacing vanished skin, more mysterious and fatal symptoms cropped up: gangrenous tonsillitis, bloody urine and numerous small subcutaneous blood spots called petechiae. Many patients began losing large amounts of hair, which fell out by the handful until the victim was bald.

"Falling hair!" Hachiya wrote in his diary. "This was an unusual symptom but undeniable. I grabbed some of my hair and pulled. I did not have much hair in the first place, but the amount that came out made me feel sick."

On August 20, Hachiya at last got a microscope, sent to

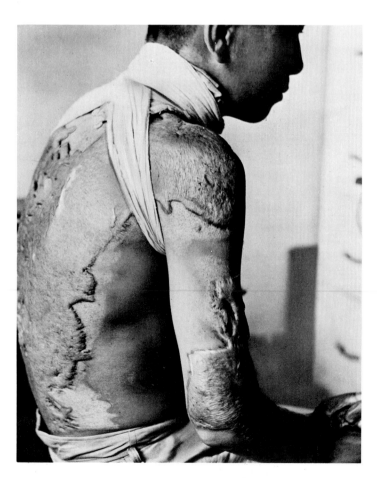

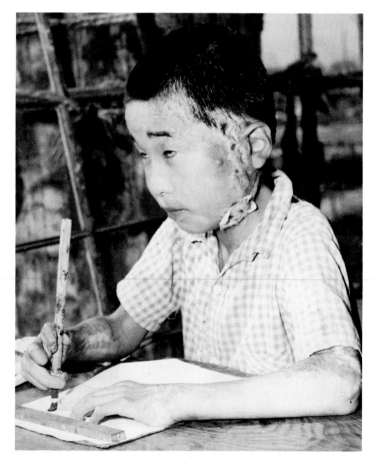

134

him all the way from Tokyo, and he immediately made some fascinating discoveries. He began by examining blood samples from six members of the staff. All had white cell counts of around 3,000, barely half the normal count. Those patients with the mysterious symptoms were found to be even worse off: Most had white cell counts around 2,000, others as low as 600. One very ill patient yielded a count of only 200, and died soon after the test was made.

Additional blood tests revealed that patients' red blood cells were abnormal and that platelets, the elements that control the blood's vital capacity to clot, were dangerously low. A series of autopsies, performed in a wooden shack near the hospital, confirmed what the blood tests had hinted at: In nearly every case, vital organs in the body had been damaged and the direct cause of death had been massive internal hemorrhage.

As the death toll from the new symptoms mounted, Dr. Hachiya and others in Hiroshima and Nagasaki became inured to the tragedy. As Hachiya wrote: "People were dying so fast that I had begun to accept death as a matter of course and ceased to respect its awfulness. I considered a family lucky if it had not lost more than two of its members."

Exactly how many were indeed lost has never been determined with strict accuracy. An initial investigation produced casualty figures of 68,670 dead and 72,880 wounded. The veracity of these figures was soon cast into doubt by the hundreds upon hundreds of bodies that continued to be found in Hiroshima's rubble. Later estimates raised the death count as a direct result of the bomb to 140,000. The carnage, of course, was most dense at the hypocenter. Of 3,483 persons known to have been within a radius of 500 yards of Ground Zero at the moment of detonation, 88 per cent died immediately or did not survive the day.

In human terms, the plutonium bomb dropped at Nagasaki proved to be a reaper not quite as lethal as its Hiroshima predecessor. Although estimates varied widely, an initial count put the dead at 37,507 and the wounded at 26,709. Later estimates raised the death toll to 70,000 by December of 1945. Nearly everyone within a 1,000-yard "circle of death" around Ground Zero died immediately or within a few hours.

But the horror of the bombs was not reflected just in the casualty lists of the times. No one could then predict the aftereffects of the radiation that permeated Hiroshima and Nagasaki. In the years and even decades that followed the appearance of the mushroom clouds, latent radiation chose new victims at random and with little warning. Hundreds of seemingly healthy people became ill and died with symptoms of radiation sickness, or from illnesses thought to be spawned by radiation. The people of Hiroshima and Nagasaki came to realize that none among them could be absolutely sure of having escaped the wrath of the nuclear explosions. Thus to the list of terrors introduced by the atomic bomb was added another: the terror of the unknown.

Two Hiroshima survivors, a man and a schoolchild, bear hypertrophic scars. These thick, rubbery overgrowths of protective skin tissue usually developed in victims who suffered the deepest flash burns.

ASSESSING THE AFTERMATH

Government officials survey the rubble of Nagasaki 24 hours after the major industrial city was obliterated by the second atomic bomb dropped on Japan.

WASTELANDS SHAPED BY UNTHINKABLE FORCE

The atomic bombs of August 1945—with a force beyond the previous comprehension of mankind—reduced Hiroshima and Nagasaki from bustling centers of war industry to blackened wastelands. "It seemed impossible," said one eyewitness, "that such a scene could have been created by human means."

In an effort to calculate the dimensions of the bombs' power, a group of Japanese scientists and engineers led by atomic physicist Yoshio Nishina probed through the ruins for days afterward, oblivious to the hazards of lingering nuclear radiation. They discovered that the air bursts had produced pressures that matched the sustained thrust of a tidal wave, knocking down all but the strongest buildings of concrete and steel. Heat, measured in thousands of degrees Fahrenheit and traveling at the speed of light, had set fire to wooden structures that were more than a mile from Ground Zero, the hypocenter above which each bomb exploded. At twice that distance, infrared rays had charred telephone poles and burned human skin.

Several miles from each hypocenter, the blast damage was still so severe that many survivors were convinced that a conventional bomb had exploded close by. "The whole city," read a Nagasaki prefectural report, "suffered damage such as would have resulted from direct hits everywhere by ordinary bombs." But anyone who doubted that a single bomb had been responsible in each city had only to consult the many clocks and watches shocked or seared to a stop at the same fateful moment.

The atomic bombs had wiped out their principal targets, completely destroying the headquarters of the Japanese Second Army in Hiroshima and reducing the Mitsubishi war plants at Nagasaki to a tangle of twisted girders. Subsequently, volumes of reports prepared by American and Japanese investigators assessed the weapons' full and sometimes inexplicable effects, but none were more telling than the few words written by officials after their inspection of Nagasaki. The city, they wrote, was "like a graveyard with not a tombstone left standing."

The hands on the scorched face of a wrist watch, found in the ashes of Hiroshima, are fused at 8:16 a.m., the moment of the city's destruction.

Half of an entrance gate still stands atop the rubble of a shrine 875 yards from the hypocenter in Nagasaki, mute testimony to the A-bomb's freakish force.

A fire storm ravages a city block in smoke-obscured Hiroshima as hurrying refugees, bundled against wind and flame, seek to escape at midday on August 6.

THE FIRE STORM'S RUINOUS PATH

Fire, even more than the blast of air, was the greatest single cause of death and destruction wrought by the atomic bombs. Closely packed houses of wood, with paper walls and woven straw floors, reacted like tinder to a blowtorch in the cosmic heat of the bombs.

In Hiroshima, a thermal wave swept out over the flat alluvial plain, setting alight the homes in its path. Into the vacuum created by its passing roared hurricane-like winds, fanning a fire storm that raged for several hours. The blast effect of the bomb started other fires by upsetting charcoal-burning stoves and rupturing electrical circuits. In all, 62,000 of Hiroshima's 90,000 buildings were destroyed.

Nagasaki was somewhat more fortunate in that the hills separating its industrial quarter from the rest of the city blocked the thermal wave, and no fire storm followed. Even so, the wave of heat instantly ignited wooden buildings within two miles of the hypocenter, and 11,500 of the city's 52,000 residences burned to the ground.

Three fire engines, including Hiroshima's only extension-ladder truck, lie in the debris 4,000 feet from Ground Zero.

Shadows burned into a wooden observation tower and outlined in chalk by investigators record a Nagasaki air-raid observer's last moments. After descending from his post by a ladder (left), he hung up his sword belt (right) and was unbuttoning his jacket when the bomb exploded.

GHOSTLY SHADOWS THAT TOLD A STORY

Professor Yoshio Nishina's first glance at Hiroshima from the air convinced him that "nothing but an atomic bomb could have done such damage." On the ground, the scientist nevertheless searched the length and breadth of the ruins to make calculations of the damage and prove beyond doubt that the elemental forces of the atom had been unleashed against Japan.

Perhaps the most telling evidence came from the sharply defined shadows of people and objects found on the scorched surfaces against which they had stood. By carefully measuring the angles at which the shadows had been cast, Nishina was able to determine precisely the height and center of the fireball that had caused the ghostly phenomenon. Then he dug up the ground directly under the point of the explosion to test its radioactivity; he also measured the thickness of scattered roof tiles melted by the heat. Putting these data together, he and other scientists made the remarkably accurate estimate—later confirmed by Allied investigators—that the bomb, which exploded at an altitude of 1,850 feet, had seared the earth beneath it with a burst of heat exceeding 5,400° F.

Concrete pillars on Yorozugo Bridge in Hiroshima cast permanent white shadows on the heat-blackened surface, more than half a mile from the point of the atomic detonation.

The angled shadow of a valve wheel is imprinted on the scorched paint of a fuel tank at the Hiroshima Gas Company. By sighting back along such shadow lines at widely separated points, surveyors calculated the center point of the explosion.

A storm-sewer drain and downspout protrude from the edge of the Aioi Bridge in Hiroshima, thrust upward by a shock wave that hit the river and rebounded

STRUCTURES SKEWED BY THE ATOMIC HAMMER

Because they were detonated hundreds of feet above the earth, the atomic bombs produced curious and unprecedented effects on the structures directly beneath. Striking vertically downward, shock waves drove the broad roofs and ceilings of reinforced concrete buildings into their basements. But the walls of the same buildings, presenting only a narrow cross section to the blast, often remained standing.

Pillars directly below the bursts were hammered into the ground like pegs; trees were stripped of their branches while the trunks remained erect. At greater distances from the hypocenter, the angle of the blast effect inclined more nearly in the direction of the horizontal, and structures leaned, tilted or were blown away.

Concrete bridges directly under the aerial shock wave displayed the most curious effects of all: Braced to resist the weight of traffic from above, they buckled upward when the tremendous force reflected instead from the water beneath them.

The upper sections of stone lanterns tilt toward the outer edges of the Motoyasu Bridge in Hiroshima, indicating that the bomb burst almost overhead and exerted nearly equal pressures downward and outward.

THE CRUSHING EFFECTS OF IMMENSE PRESSURE

Reinforced concrete buildings caught by the gigantic force of the atomic explosions yielded to pressures never envisioned by their earthquake-conscious Japanese designers. Nor were the effects of conventional blockbuster bombs any precedent, for the peak pressures of such bombs dissipated after a few milliseconds, punching holes in their targets but leaving major portions of the structures intact.

The atomic bombs exerted pressures exceeding 4.6 tons per square yard that lasted as long as a second and traveled at twice the speed of sound. This force had the effect, engineers found, "of a powerful push which shoved buildings over or left them leaning."

Investigations after the War by American engineers showed that "small buildings were virtually engulfed in the pressure wave and simultaneously crushed from different directions." Even at great distances, roofs and walls that faced the explosions "were completely wracked."

Sections of a metal drainpipe point away from the blast center.

Sited along a radius to the explosion in Nagasaki, an interior wall remains standing after the broadside portions of a two-story building were blown away.

As a freakish result of the blast pressure, the second story and clock tower of a concrete building stand tilted but intact after the first floor collapsed.

SKELETONS OF TWISTED STEEL

Even massive, steel-framed factory buildings bowed and bent under the one-two punch of the atomic fireballs and shock waves. Curiously, factories sheathed with corrugated iron plates or sheet-metal walls and roofs suffered greater damage than those covered with flimsier fibrous materials like asbestos siding.

The lighter material simply crumbled, letting the shock waves pass through the steel skeleton. "But the steel siding," engineers later reported, "transferred the pressure to the structural members, causing distortion or general collapse."

Railroad tracks and trestles also twisted under the pressures of heat and shock, impeding survivors who tried to use them to escape from the burning cities.

A twisted steel pylon (top) in Nagasaki and the frame of a Hiroshima factory building (below) lean away from the direction of the bombs' shock waves.

Enormous girders are bent like putty at the Mitsubishi steelworks in Nagasaki, and metal equipment clutters the floor under the skeleton of the roof.

Distorted by heat and blast waves, a streetcar trestle offers pedestrians a precarious exit from the five-square-mile zone of total destruction at Hiroshima.

5

At 11 a.m. on August 9, 1945, Japanese Prime Minister Kantaro Suzuki convened an emergency meeting of the six-man Supreme Council for the Direction of the War. The council members, known as the Big Six, had been mightily shaken by the atomic bomb dropped on Hiroshima three days before. Now they had a new calamity to contend with: Earlier that morning, 1.6 million Soviet troops had stormed into Japanese-held Manchuria, dashing hopes that Moscow might lead Japan into a tolerable negotiated peace. Suzuki intended to use the meeting to propose that Japan accept the surrender ultimatum that had been issued by the Allies in late July.

"We cannot carry on this war indefinitely," said the elderly Prime Minister. "There is no way left for us but to accept the Potsdam Proclamation."

General Korechika Anami, the War Minister, responded angrily to Suzuki's proposal. "Who can be one hundred per cent sure of defeat?" he asked. "We certainly can't swallow this proclamation." With that statement, the line was drawn between the members of the Big Six who desired peace and those who demanded continued resistance, no matter how costly.

The militants—General Anami, Navy Chief of Staff Soemu Toyoda and Army Chief of Staff Yoshijiro Umezu—clung to the desperate hope that somehow, perhaps through heavenly intervention, Japan would repel the Americans, just as an unseasonable typhoon—the *Kamikaze,* or Divine Wind—had repelled a fleet of invading Mongol ships in the year 1281.

The peace faction was equally convinced that nothing in heaven or on earth could save Japan. These three men—Prime Minister Suzuki, Navy Minister Mitsumasa Yonai and Foreign Minister Shigenori Togo—viewed the Soviet invasion of Manchuria as an opportunity to silence their strident colleagues.

General Anami reminded the council of Japan's defense plan, *Ketsu Go*—Operation *Decision*—and reviewed the arithmetic of what the military could commit to repel an invasion: 53 infantry divisions and 25 brigades plus 250,000 garrison troops for a total of 2,350,000 men; in addition, the commanders could call on four million Army and Navy civilian employees for combat duty. Furthermore, the Cabinet had recently approved a measure extending the draft to

"BEARING THE UNBEARABLE"

include men from 15 to 60 and women from 17 to 45, which would bring an additional 28 million people to the country's defense.

Foreign Minister Togo demanded evidence that even so great a number of defenders could stall or turn back a landing by the American forces. Instead he received platitudes. "With luck, we will repulse the invaders before they land," said General Umezu. "At any rate, I can say with confidence that we will be able to destroy the major part of an invading force."

The Foreign Minister was scornful; even if Japanese forces managed to repel the first landing, he said, the American troops would simply come again and again until they were successful.

Arguments raged back and forth between the opposing factions for two hours until, finally, an exasperated Suzuki broke off the meeting to attend a conference of the full Cabinet, which was to debate the same issue that divided the Big Six.

Even before he opened the Cabinet meeting, Suzuki knew it would be a waste of time. A unanimous vote of the Cabinet was required to accept the Potsdam Proclamation. And General Anami, who as War Minister held Cabinet rank, was certain to reject any peace proposal. The Cabinet Ministers and their secretaries had barely taken their seats when an officer entered the meeting room and stammered out the news of still another disaster: Nagasaki had suffered the same fate as Hiroshima.

So began six torturous days in the experience of a people who in all their recorded history had never known defeat. Now the fate of 100 million Japanese had to be decided quickly lest the Americans drop a third atomic bomb. It was a time of desperation. A heroic figure was needed to quash the bickering and save the nation from destruction. Such a savior did swiftly emerge—and from a quarter so unexpected as to stun the nation.

The savior was the Emperor himself, Hirohito, 124th in a line that could be traced back to the Seventh Century A.D. Hirohito reigned but did not rule. He was venerated as a descendant of Amaterasu, the sun goddess, and as one who "lived beyond the clouds" he did not concern himself with such worldly matters as war or peace. But in Japan's dire hour of crisis, Hirohito, a slight and shy man 44 years of age who wore thick glasses and preferred to occupy himself with the study of marine biology, stepped forward to lead his people.

What forced the Emperor to act was the obvious inability of the Cabinet to do anything but wrangle. The dreadful news of Nagasaki did nothing to clarify the thinking. The Cabinet had come to order at 2:30 p.m. Just before 10 p.m., after hours of fruitless debate, Suzuki called for a vote. Most of the ministers elected to accept the Potsdam Proclamation, but there were some holdouts, notably War Minister Anami. In disgust, Suzuki adjourned the meeting, then hurried with Foreign Minister Togo to report to the Emperor. That morning, Hirohito had listened to his Prime Minister and his closest adviser, Marquis Kido, Lord Keeper of the Privy Seal, argue that the throne might have to act to break the deadlock; the latest report only deepened the impression that Japan's leaders had entangled themselves in a Gordian knot. If Japan was to have peace, Hirohito realized, he would have to be the sword that cut the knot.

Hirohito agreed to call an imperial conference that same night to end the impasse. Shortly before 11 p.m., each member of the Cabinet and the Supreme Council received a summons to attend the conference, as did Marquis Kido and several former Prime Ministers. The men were puzzled: Ordinarily they gathered in the Emperor's presence only when they were ready to present him with a unanimous decision. They hurried to the underground complex on the palace grounds adjacent to the *obunko*, or library, a reinforced concrete building. The imperial family had been living there since May, when part of the palace was destroyed in an air raid.

The room set aside for the imperial conference, an 18-by-30-foot bomb shelter, was poorly lit and virtually unventilated. The conferees, sweltering in their formal attire, found breathing difficult. At 11:50, Hirohito, looking rumpled and extremely tired, entered and took his place on a small dais between a gilt screen and a table draped in gold brocade, the only spots of color in the dark, wood-paneled room. The conferees, as tradition dictated, avoided looking directly at the revered personage who sat facing them.

Suzuki opened the conference by asking for a reading of the Potsdam Proclamation. Each member of the Big Six then rose in turn to state his views. Calm and unhurried, Foreign Minister Togo said that the time had come to end the War—if the Allies would allow Japan to keep the Emperor. Navy Minister Yonai agreed. General Anami did not. Sternly, he spelled out his conditions for peace: Japan must be permitted to demobilize its own forces, try its own alleged war criminals and impose limits on any Allied occupation. "If not, we must continue fighting with courage and find life in death."

When someone asked if Japan still had the capacity to fight, General Umezu, the Army Chief of Staff, answered with astonishing optimism: Antiaircraft measures, he asserted, could prevent further atomic-bomb attacks. "We have been preserving our strength," he said, "and we expect to counterattack."

It was 2 a.m. and nothing had been accomplished. Then the elderly Suzuki laboriously rose to his feet. "We have been discussing this matter many hours without reaching a conclusion," he began. The old voice was firm. "We have no precedent—and I find it difficult to do—but with the greatest reverence I must now ask the Emperor to express his wishes."

Slowly, he turned and began to approach the sovereign. This was close to sacrilege. There were gasps throughout the room and Anami, aghast, cried, "Mister Prime Minister!" Seeming not to hear, Suzuki kept on until he reached Hirohito's dais. There he bowed low. With an understanding nod, Hirohito gestured to Suzuki to return to his seat.

The Emperor stood and began to speak. His reedy voice revealed the stress he felt at breaking with centuries of tradition. "I have given serious thought," he said, "to the situation prevailing at home and abroad and have concluded that continuing the War means destruction for the nation and a prolongation of bloodshed and cruelty in the world."

His listeners were silent, mesmerized.

"I cannot bear to see my innocent people suffer any longer." Hirohito paused, stared toward the steel-beamed ceiling and wiped his glasses with white-gloved fingers. He spoke again. "It pains me to think of those who served me so faithfully, the soldiers and sailors who have been killed or wounded in far-off battles, the families who have lost all their worldly goods—and often their lives as well."

The Emperor was not supposed to have to say these things, to endure the pain of giving voice to what they all knew: that Japan had risked everything—and lost. By speaking, Hirohito had tapped a well of powerful emotion ordinarily hidden behind formally impassive faces. Several men in the room were slumped in their seats, heads down, shoulders heaving.

The Emperor went on. "The time has come when we must bear the unbearable. I swallow my tears and give my sanction to the proposal to accept the Allied proclamation on the basis outlined by the Foreign Minister."

Hirohito turned and walked from the room. By dawn on the morning of August 10, each Cabinet member had signed a statement accepting the Potsdam Proclamation— on the condition that "the supreme power of the Emperor" not be compromised.

By the time the rest of Japan awakened, cables announcing the imperial conference's conditional agreement were on their way to Tokyo's embassies in Switzerland and Sweden; from there, the news would be forwarded to Washington, Moscow, London and Chungking.

Marquis Koichi Kido, Hirohito's closest adviser, relaxes outdoors with a cup of tea. As early as February 1942, the pragmatic 52-year-old aristocrat realized that Japan could not win and urged the Emperor "to grasp any opportunity to terminate the War."

At 9:30 that morning, General Anami entered the War Ministry on Ichigaya Heights to inform his staff of the decision to capitulate. "I do not know what excuse I can offer," Anami said to a group of 50 officers gathered in an air-raid bunker. "But since it is the wish of His Imperial Majesty that we accept the Potsdam Proclamation, there is nothing that can be done." When several officers started to protest, Anami cut them off. "Your individual feelings and those of the men under you must be disregarded," he said. Then, slapping his riding crop against his palm for emphasis, the War Minister concluded, "If anyone here wishes to act contrary to His Majesty's decision, he will have to do so over my dead body."

Anami's declaration did not stifle the spirit of all his officers. Later that day, two of them—including his own brother-in-law, Lieut. Colonel Masahiko Takeshita—managed to have a message broadcast in Anami's name urging troops all over Japan's shrinking Empire to "fight resolutely, even though we may have to chew grass, eat dirt and sleep in the fields."

When Foreign Minister Togo learned of the bogus message, he decided not to wait for the imperial conference's decision to reach the Allies through official channels. If he did not contact Washington immediately, he feared, the Allies might construe the insubordinate officers' exhortation as an official rejection of the Potsdam Proclamation. That evening, the Foreign Minister persuaded an editor of the Domei news agency to beam the imperial conference's statement directly to the United States and Europe in English, using Morse code.

Even as the message went out, a group of rebellious Army officers exploded grenades in Tokyo, hoping to provoke the imposition of martial law and strengthen the Army's grip. They failed; in a city reeling from months of continuous bombing, nobody paid much attention to a few grenades.

Across the world, Togo's radio message was picked up on August 10 at 7:30 a.m., Washington time. President Truman, when informed of the message, summoned four key aides—Secretary of State Byrnes, Secretary of War Stimson, Secretary of the Navy James V. Forrestal and Admiral William Leahy, Chairman of the Joint Chiefs of Staff. The message itself was clear:

"The Japanese government is ready to accept the terms enumerated in the joint declaration issued at Potsdam on July 26, 1945, with an understanding that the said declaration does not compromise any demand which prejudices the prerogatives of His Majesty as a sovereign ruler."

Truman asked his aides for their opinions. He had been demanding surrender without conditions and yet the Japanese had stubbornly imposed one. Stimson voted for keeping Hirohito in place, arguing that his cooperation would be needed to ensure the surrender of all Japanese forces. "Something like this use of the Emperor must be made to save us from a score of bloody Iwo Jimas," the Secretary of War said. Leahy and Forrestal nodded agreement, but Byrnes was skeptical. "If any conditions are to be accepted," said the Secretary of State, "I want the U.S. and not Japan to state the conditions."

Truman decided to adjourn the meeting to await Japan's message through official channels; meanwhile, Byrnes was to draft a response. Shortly after noon, the message arrived and the President convened a full Cabinet meeting to hear Byrnes's proposed answer.

"From the moment of surrender," the Secretary of State had written, "the authority of the Emperor and the Japanese Government to rule the state shall be subject to the Supreme Commander of the Allied powers, who will take such steps as he deems necessary to effectuate the surrender terms." Byrnes added that "the ultimate form of government of Japan will be established by the freely expressed will of the Japanese people."

With that masterlily worded message, Byrnes had reassured the Japanese that *kokutai*—the national essence as embodied in the Emperor—would be preserved. And he had done so without making an absolute commitment. Impressed, Truman approved the message and ordered the State Department to submit it to the Allies for approval.

All but Russia accepted immediately. The Soviets were greedy. They had been at war with Japan for only two days and they needed more time to swallow up all the territory that Stalin coveted—Manchuria, North Korea, the Kurile Islands and Sakhalin island. To stall the peace offensive, the Soviets insisted that they share the Allied high command in occupied Japan and demanded veto power over the selection of a supreme commander.

A LAST-MINUTE GRAB FOR SPOILS

A Soviet biplane scouts overhead as tanks of the Trans-Baikal Area Army roll across the sandy Mongolian plains toward Manchuria in August of 1945.

At midnight on August 8, the Soviet Union entered the Pacific war with a vengeance. From east, north and west about 1.6 million troops and 3,000 tanks stormed into Manchuria. Soviet planes—almost 6,000 of them—backed the invasion by striking against Japanese convoys and cities in Manchuria and Korea, a Japanese protectorate. The Soviet Pacific Fleet stood ready to carry the invasion to islands north of Japan: south Sakhalin and the Kuriles, which Czarist Russia had lost to Japan 40 years earlier in the War of 1904-1905.

Opposing the Russians was the once-mighty Kwantung Army—fully a third of its remaining 600,000 men newly drafted civilians. The Japanese had no modern antitank weapons and only obsolescent artillery, for which there were few shells.

The defenders' best weapon was foul weather. Relentless rain limited Soviet air sorties and turned Manchuria's few roads to muck. Soviet tanks striking out of Mongolia managed with considerable difficulty to cross rivers swollen by the seasonal downpours—only to run out of fuel when their supply trucks became mired in the Manchurian plain. Whenever the weather cleared, airdrops supplied the fuel the Red Army needed to drive on to the Manchurian city of Changchun.

The one-sided fighting went on officially until September 1—sixteen days after the Emperor's surrender broadcast. By then the Soviets had carried the invasion to within about 100 miles of Peking, linking up with Mao Tse-tung's Chinese Communists and giving them captured Japanese arms. In all, according to Soviet reports, some 80,000 Japanese and 8,200 Russian soldiers were killed.

The victors took home everything they could move. They dismantled steel mills and other industrial plants and used the 16,000 cars and 2,000 locomotives of the confiscated Manchurian railroad to ship their booty to the Soviet Union. They also captured more than 600,000 military and civilian prisoners—most of whom disappeared behind the Iron Curtain, never to return home again.

Sailors of the Soviet Pacific Fleet display their flag over the bay at Port Arthur in southern Manchuria. A Soviet force occupied the ice-free port, visible in the background, which had fallen to Japan in 1905 after a four-month siege.

Backed by a submachine gunner, a Red Army officer awaits Japanese envoys, carrying a white flag of surrender, on a bridge near the town of Tungliao.

In a predawn meeting with Foreign Minister Vyacheslav M. Molotov, the American Ambassador to Moscow, W. Averell Harriman, brusquely rejected the Soviet demands, saying they were "utterly out of the question." A few hours later, realizing their bid had failed, the Soviets backed down and agreed to Byrnes's message. On August 12, the Allies sent their official reply through the Swiss and also broadcast the message via short wave from San Francisco.

In Tokyo, Marquis Kido rushed a transcript of the message to the *obunko* and read it to the Emperor, stressing the clause calling for Japan's ultimate form of government to be set "by the freely expressed will of the people." That, he pointed out, could conceivably mean the end of the monarchy. "That is beside the point," Hirohito said. "It would be useless if the people did not want an emperor. I think it's perfectly all right to leave it up to the people."

But when the Cabinet met to discuss the Allied broadcast, matters slid swiftly into the impasse of three days earlier. Togo spoke in favor of accepting the enemy reply. If Japan insisted on further revisions, the Allies might abolish the imperial dynasty outright instead of leaving the decision to the Japanese people.

General Anami stood and demanded that the Allied reply be rejected. "They are proposing to thwart the Sovereign's prerogative," he said. "I maintain that we fight on to the bitter end in defense of *kokutai*."

Support for Anami was forthcoming from a guest at the meeting, Baron Kiichiro Hiranuma, the President of the Privy Council, which advised the Emperor on matters of state. The 78-year-old former Prime Minister argued that making the Emperor subject to the Supreme Commander of the Allied powers meant virtual slavery for Hirohito. Hiranuma had no vote in Cabinet proceedings, but his impassioned rhetoric won over two of the ministers. Even Suzuki seemed to cave in during the heated debate. "If disarmament is forced upon us," he said, "we have no alternative but to continue the War."

Togo was stunned by Suzuki's reversal. The Foreign Minister decided the meeting had better end before the move toward peace collapsed entirely. At his urging, Suzuki adjourned the meeting.

Togo returned to his office and told an aide that he might have to resign if the Cabinet continued to bicker. The aide, Vice Minister Shunichi Matsumoto, advised Togo to play for time. The official Allied reply had just arrived at the Swiss Embassy. "Why don't we pretend it didn't arrive until tomorrow morning?" Matsumoto suggested. "Tonight, please go home and rest." Togo agreed, pausing only long enough to telephone Marquis Kido to inform him that things were falling apart.

That evening the Lord Keeper of the Privy Seal summoned Suzuki to his office. He intended to stiffen the Prime Minister's resolve to fight for peace. "Should we turn down the Potsdam Proclamation at this stage," Kido told Suzuki, "a million innocent Japanese would die from bombings and starvation. If we bring about peace now, four or five of us might be assassinated, but it would be worth it. Furthermore, it is His Majesty's wish."

Kido's fervor carried the day. "Yes, let us do it," Suzuki exclaimed, adding that he would stand firm against the militant faction. Kido had accurately sensed the Prime Minister's thoughts; by reassuring Suzuki that the Emperor desired peace at all costs, Kido had brought the Prime Minister back into the peace faction. The Keeper of the Privy Seal had also accurately read the winds of dissent that were

Lieut. Colonel Masahiko Takeshita, a firebrand leader in the plot to thwart Japan's capitulation, wears the golden braids of a staff officer in this 1945 photograph. Takeshita later made his peace with the Occupation and became a general in Japan's postwar Ground Self-Defense Force.

swirling about the War Ministry. The previous day, a group of young officers had marked him and other members of the peace group for assassination as part of a coup d'état aimed at continuing the War.

On August 11, inside a sweltering bomb shelter in the War Ministry, 15 Army and Navy officers had met to plot rebellion. They were led by Anami's brother-in-law, Takeshita, and by a fiery young major named Kenji Hatanaka. Takeshita, who was aware of the deliberations of the Big Six through his relationship with Anami, began the meeting by pointing out that Suzuki, Togo and Kido would have to be assassinated. With the leading peace advocates out of the way, said Takeshita, "I guarantee that General Anami will join us."

The War Minister's participation was the key to the rebellion. The conspirators believed that if they won over someone like Anami, other leaders—among them the commander of the Army forces around Tokyo and the commander of the Palace Guard—would join forces with them. With the Palace Guard under their control, the rebels were convinced that they could isolate the Emperor and persuade him to continue the War.

Over the next two days, the rebels tried repeatedly to approach Anami; each time he managed to avoid them. The War Minister sympathized with his young officers, but he felt bound by the Emperor's wishes to end the War. Time seemed to be running out on the conspirators. On the morning of August 13, Hatanaka and Takeshita took up a vigil at Anami's home; they would remain until they had his answer.

Meanwhile, Anami was on his way to a meeting of the Big Six to discuss the American proposal anew. When he arrived at the palace, he found the peace faction united once more; Prime Minister Suzuki was puffing on a cigar and arguing vigorously for peace. The morning dragged by in futile debate. At noon, the Prime Minister ended the Big Six meeting to prepare for a Cabinet meeting that afternoon and what he expected would be another bout of futile bickering.

He was not disappointed; the only break in the arguing came when a messenger burst in with a copy of an Army communiqué that was to be released to the radio network and the newspapers at 4 p.m.: "The Army, upon receipt of a newly issued imperial command, has renewed offensive action against the United States, the United Kingdom, the Soviet Union and China."

Obviously, the rebels had been busy. "I don't know anything about this," Anami shouted. He immediately telephoned General Umezu at the War Ministry, where the equally startled Chief of Staff managed to have the announcement quashed only minutes before it would have been broadcast throughout the Empire.

When the excitement over the bogus communiqué had died down, Suzuki called for a vote on whether to accept the official American reply to Japan's surrender offer. Without the presence of Admiral Toyoda and General Umezu—who were not members of the Cabinet—to support Anami, the Prime Minister felt he could isolate the War Minister as the sole dissenter and perhaps persuade him to change his vote. The tactic failed; 12 ministers declared for peace, but both the Home Affairs Minister and the Justice Minister sided with Anami.

Exasperated beyond endurance, Suzuki adjourned the Cabinet session with the warning that if the impasse were not soon broken, he would have to ask the Emperor for one final decision. Anami pleaded with him for a delay of two days, so he could try to prevent the Army from rebelling. "I'm sorry," Suzuki said. "This is our golden opportunity and we must seize it."

The War Minister left the room and Suzuki turned to his doctor, who had stayed close at hand throughout the day in case the aged Prime Minister's health should fail under the strain of round-the-clock negotiations. "If we delay," Suzuki explained, "the Russians may occupy Hokkaido. This would deal the country a fatal blow."

"But General Anami might kill himself," Suzuki's physician protested.

"I know," the Prime Minister replied. "I'm sorry."

When Anami returned to his home at 8 o'clock in the morning, he found his brother-in-law, Hatanaka and eight other young officers waiting to see him. Japan must not surrender, they exclaimed; the peace advocates were to be arrested, the palace isolated and martial law proclaimed. The War Minister professed sympathy, but he remained noncommittal. He told the young officers he would meet again with their representative at midnight; but at the midnight meeting Anami again deferred his decision until the following day, August 14.

While Hatanaka and the other rebels argued with General Anami, his cohorts on the Big Six, General Umezu and Admiral Toyoda, were pleading their case against accepting the Allies' terms with Foreign Minister Togo. The meeting ended abruptly when Admiral Takajiro Onishi, creator of the Kamikaze Corps, burst into the room. Onishi was in tears and practically hysterical.

"We must submit a plan to gain victory to His Majesty," Onishi blurted. "We must throw ourselves headlong into the plan. If we are prepared to sacrifice 20 million Japanese lives, victory will be ours." He was interrupted by the wail of air-raid sirens. The War was still going on. Admiral Halsey's carrier planes had struck Tokyo earlier in the day, and now General Spaatz's B-29s were overhead.

When Onishi tried to continue, Togo cut him off. "Winning one battle," he said, "will not win the War for us." With that rebuke, Foreign Minister Togo left the palace; Onishi's outburst had made him more determined than ever to bring matters to a head the next day.

August 14 began with a message from the Americans. Tokyo residents who awoke near dawn saw a lone B-29 overhead. The plane was carrying a nonlethal payload, leaflets that said in part: "American planes are not dropping bombs on you today. They are dropping leaflets instead because the Japanese government has offered to surrender and every Japanese has a right to know the terms."

Marquis Kido picked up one of the leaflets on the palace grounds and was alarmed by what he read. He hurried to the Emperor and warned him there might be a general rebellion if the troops got hold of the leaflets. Hirohito realized that time was running out. He would wait no longer for a Cabinet decision, but on his own authority would summon an imperial conference of the entire Cabinet for 10:30 a.m. If there were still signs of dissension or hesitation, he said, "I will command surrender."

Wearing a simple Army uniform, Hirohito entered the underground conference chamber at 10:50 that morning. Suzuki opened the meeting by asking for opinions. Again there were disagreements. Then the Emperor spoke: "If there are no more opinions, I will express mine," he said. He was formal and polite, as protocol required, but this time he left no doubt that he was commanding acquiescence. "I want you all to agree with my conclusions. We cannot continue the War any longer," he went on. "I realize full well how difficult it will be for the loyal officers and men of the Army and Navy to surrender their arms to the enemy and see their country occupied and perhaps stand accused as war criminals." Hirohito's self-control broke for a moment and he wiped tears from his cheeks. Two of the ministers fell to the floor weeping. Hirohito continued: "It is my desire that all of you, my ministers of state, bow to my wishes and accept the Allied reply forthwith. It is my desire that

the Cabinet at once draw up an Imperial Rescript to end the War.'' He walked out, leaving his ministers to sort out their emotions.

The Emperor had left them no room for doubt or maneuver, and even General Anami at last seemed resigned. The paramount remaining question was how to spread the word. During the conference, Hirohito had offered to go anywhere, do anything, even make a radio broadcast if it would speed the peace. This, too, was without precedent; the nation had never heard the Emperor's voice on the air except once briefly in 1928 when, by an acoustical freak, a microphone had picked up an imperial conversation from 50 yards away.

Meeting through the afternoon at Prime Minister Suzuki's official residence, the Cabinet drafted the imperial rescript that would bring an end to the War. Two copyists, working with brushes and ink, then began the painstaking task of setting down the 815 characters of the rescript in formal court language. The ministers agreed that an imperial broadcast was necessary. The Emperor, they reasoned, was the only person the people would believe and obey. But the ministers balked at the prospect of putting their venerated leader on the air live, and they decided to have him record his broadcast instead.

At 2 p.m. Anami had appeared at the War Ministry to inform his subordinates. ''His Majesty has rendered his final decision in favor of terminating the War,'' said the War Minister, fighting back tears as he spoke. ''The Imperial Army must act in complete accord with this decision.''

Major Hatanaka began to weep; another officer asked Anami, ''Why have you lost your resolve?''

Anami closed his eyes for a moment, then spoke: ''I could not refuse the Emperor any longer. Especially, when he asked, in tears, to bear the pain no matter how trying it might be. I could not but forget everything and accept it.''

Several officers wept openly as they left the Ministry; others, among them Major Hatanaka, departed vowing to stage their coup even without Anami's support.

Meanwhile, the two copyists had finished the rescript. When the document was taken to Hirohito, he asked for minor changes. Because time was running short, the alterations were brushed on separate slips of paper and pasted to the text. Thus the historic document had become a sort of

parchment jigsaw puzzle by the time Hirohito signed it at 8:30 that evening. Getting the signatures of all the Cabinet members used up additional time, and it was 11 p.m. before preparations for the Emperor's recording were completed.

A short time later, the Foreign Ministry sent a note to the Allied nations through the embassies in Switzerland and Sweden notifying them that Japan had accepted their conditions of surrender.

At 11:30, the Emperor appeared at an improvised studio that had been set up in the Household Ministry. There, before an awed but weary crew of Radio Tokyo technicians who had been waiting for him since midafternoon, Hirohito recorded the rescript twice. The first time he stumbled over a few phrases. The second time his voice was too shrill and he omitted a word. He offered to make a third recording, but a royal chamberlain, Yoshihiro Tokugawa, demurred, believing another session to be too much of an ordeal to ask of the royal personage. Hirohito left to return to the *obunko* and a night's rest.

After Hirohito had departed, someone asked what to do with the two 10-inch phonograph records until they could be broadcast the next day. Rumors of a possible Army uprising lent urgency to the question. At length, Tokugawa put the records in a cloth bag and locked them in a small safe in an office used by the Empress Nagako's retinue. As an extra precaution, Tokugawa heaped papers over the safe to obscure it.

Tokugawa had acted just in time; Hatanaka intended to occupy the palace grounds within a few hours, destroy the Emperor's recordings and plead with him to continue the War. The wildly aggressive young major had failed to gain high-level support for his coup, but he had won the backing of several officers of the Palace Guard. He believed that the

Emperor Hirohito meets with his ministers in an underground room on the 14th of August, 1945, in order to express his firm desire to end the War. Prime Minister Kantaro Suzuki (far left, front row) provided artist Ichiro Shirakawa with the description on which this painting is based.

Superimposed on one of the two 10-inch discs on which Hirohito recorded his surrender broadcast is a copy of his address, composed in a formal court grammar that only the Emperor was permitted to use.

rest would surely follow if he could win the support of their commander, General Takeshi Mori—or convince the others that he had done so.

Shortly after 1:30 a.m., Hatanaka and two conspirators cornered General Mori in his office just inside the palace grounds. One of Hatanaka's accomplices, Colonel Masataka Ida, had been pleading with the general for more than an hour to sanction the rebellion. Mori, who was torn between his desire to continue fighting and his loyalty to the Emperor, had stalled, trying to avoid making a commitment. Mori was running out of arguments; Hatanaka had already run out of patience.

Hatanaka demanded an immediate answer, but Mori refused. "I'm not sure what is right," he said. "I would like to go to the Meiji Shrine"—the nearby Shinto holy place—"where I can cleanse myself of all impure thoughts. Then I can tell who is correct."

Hatanaka's self-control broke at Mori's answer. "This is a waste of time," he shouted. One of his men took that as a signal for action and drew his sword. An aide moved to protect General Mori and was struck down; a second conspirator beheaded the man where he lay. Now there was a pistol in Hatanaka's hand and he fired. Mori fell dead.

Hatanaka staggered out of the office, weapon in hand, and muttered to Ida, "I did it because there was no time left. I'm sorry." Regretful or not, Hatanaka quickly put the murder to practical use. He appropriated the dead general's personal seal and used it to forge orders to close off the palace grounds and to occupy the headquarters of NHK, the national broadcast corporation, in order to prevent the Emperor's rescript from going on the air.

At 4 a.m. a company of men took over the NHK building, while the Palace Guard sealed the palace grounds—shutting the great iron gates, cutting telephone lines and placing machine guns at strategic points. The radio technicians who had recorded the imperial rescript were stopped as they tried to leave. Under heavy questioning, one technician ad-

With a bow taller than himself, War Minister Korechika Anami practices archery, a traditional samurai exercise. When the 58-year-old general committed suicide a few hours before Hirohito announced Japan's surrender, he left behind the blood-spattered note (above) in which he apologized for what he called his "great crime."

mitted that he had given the recordings to a court chamberlain, whom he described to his captors as "a tall man with a big nose." Actually, Tokugawa, the man who had cached the recordings, was a short man with a snub nose; the technician's lie would keep the chamberlain and the recordings out of harm's way throughout the frantic morning.

Meanwhile, Hatanaka had sent Colonel Ida off on another mission crucial to the coup: He was to seek the support of General Shizuichi Tanaka, an Oxford-educated officer who, as commander of the Eastern District Army, had authority over all troops in the Tokyo area. Ida returned with disheartening news: "Eastern District won't go along," he said. In fact, Tanaka's Chief of Staff, General Tatsuhiko Takashima, had ordered Ida to withdraw all troops from the palace grounds.

Takashima's rebuke had cooled Ida's zeal, and he tried to persuade Hatanaka to end the rebellion. "If you try to force this thing, there will be chaos," he argued. "Face the facts. The coup has failed."

"I understand," nodded Hatanaka, all the color drained from his face.

But when Ida departed, Hatanaka became combative again. When General Takashima telephoned him at the Palace Guard's barracks, he pleaded his case anew. "Please understand our ardor," Hatanaka begged, his voice cracking. Takashima answered that he could understand Hatanaka's feelings but that the Emperor's command had to be obeyed. "We have reached the point where the final outcome cannot be changed," he said coldly. "Hatanaka, do you understand me?"

Hatanaka did not answer, but his sobbing was audible over the wire before he slammed down the telephone. He was not beaten yet. His troops still occupied the palace grounds; they also controlled the NHK building and its broadcast facilities. If he held the radio station, he could prevent the Emperor's message from being broadcast as scheduled later that day.

Colonel Ida, meanwhile, had decided to inform General Anami of the night's developments. When he reached the War Minister's home, he found Anami and his brother-in-law, Takeshita, chatting amiably over a bottle of sake. Several hours earlier, Takeshita had made a final attempt to sway his kinsman to join the coup. Anami again had turned him down, telling him that he could not disobey the Emperor, but that he would commit suicide before the broadcast. Touched, Takeshita abandoned all thoughts of rebellion in order to remain with Anami.

"Come in," Anami said cheerfully to Ida. "I am getting ready to die."

"I think it would be fine," said Ida, adding that the War Minister's suicide would end any doubts the Army might have about surrendering. "I will join you shortly."

Anami slapped Ida sharply across the face. His own suicide would be enough, he said. Ida had to stay alive "for the future of Japan."

As the night progressed, Anami began preparing for his death. He selected a pair of ceremonial daggers, giving one to Takeshita "to remember me by." He pinned his medals to his dress uniform and draped a white shirt over his torso. "This was given to me by the Emperor," Anami said. "He had worn it himself. I intend to die wearing it."

At 4 a.m., Anami declared, "I will go now." Ida and Takeshita bowed themselves out of the room. Alone, Anami went into a corridor and sat facing the Imperial Palace. He plunged his dagger into his abdomen at the left side, then drew it across to the right and thrust upward. This was the classic rite of seppuku, a death so painful that few could summon the courage to perform it. Anami withdrew the dagger from his stomach and probed with its point to find the carotid artery under his ear, hoping to speed his death. He was still upright when Takeshita returned, bent over him and murmured, "Can I help you?"

"No need," Anami gasped. "Go away." He was still sitting erectly on his haunches when his groans brought Takeshita back. Takeshita took the dagger from Anami's grasp and drove it deep into his brother-in-law's neck.

Even as General Anami sat dying, a group of soldiers and engineering students in Yokohama commandeered several vehicles and were traveling toward Tokyo intent on assassinating all members of the Cabinet peace faction. The men, who called themselves the Kokumin Kamikaze Tai—the National Divine Wind Corps—were armed with pistols, swords and two light machine guns. Their first target was Prime Minister Suzuki, whom their leader, Captain Takeo Sasaki, had labeled an archtraitor.

Dawn was just breaking when the expedition pulled up at the gate of the Prime Minister's official residence. Sasaki opened up with his machine guns. Inside, a few exhausted officials, including Cabinet Secretary Hisatsune Sakomizu, were awakened by the thud of bullets and fled to safety through an underground passage. When Sasaki stormed the gate to finish the job, a guard told him that Suzuki was not there but was sleeping at his private home. Sasaki set the official residence afire, gathered his crew and headed for Suzuki's home.

In the Suzuki house the telephone shrilled and the Prime Minister's son, Hajime, picked it up. A man whom Hajime took to be a policeman or soldier told him that Sasaki was on the way. "Warn him," the man said. "Tell him to leave at once." Hajime ran to his father and helped him dress. Then Hajime and his parents hurried to their official car, which was parked outside. The car failed to start. Seeing the predicament, the police guards stationed at Suzuki's home rushed up and began pushing the car downhill; under their impetus the engine finally turned over. The Suzukis reached the highway and drove away moments before the assassins arrived.

Frustrated at having missed the Prime Minister, Sasaki torched his house as consolation. He then led his men to the home of Baron Hiranuma, President of the Privy Council. Again, Sasaki and his gang failed to draw blood; the aging nobleman had fled to safety before their arrival. Sasaki set the baron's mansion ablaze. Then, their spleen vented, Sasaki and his ragtag group headed home to Yokohama.

At about the same time, Major Hatanaka, pedaling furiously on an old bicycle, reached the NHK building, determined to go on the air himself to raise support for his rebellion. When Hatanaka demanded at gunpoint to take over a microphone, the engineers stalled him. First they told him that they could not broadcast without special permission from Army headquarters; then they told him they would need time to prepare a national radio hookup.

At that point, a telephone rang. It was General Takashima. Hatanaka took the telephone to plead for a few minutes on the air. Suddenly, he stopped talking. "Your situation is hopeless," Takashima told him. "You are like soldiers trying to defend a position in a cave with no way out." Hatanaka put down the telephone, wiped his eyes and turned to his followers. "Let's go," he said. The revolt was sputtering out.

At about dawn, a chamberlain named Yasuhide Toda persuaded Hatanaka's men—who remained in control at the palace grounds—to let him into the *obunko*, where the Emperor had slept the night away unaware that he was a prisoner. Toda feared that dissident troops milling around the palace grounds might enter the bunker to search for the recordings. He had come to help the Emperor escape.

At 6:40 a.m., Hirohito appeared in a dressing gown and Toda told him what had occurred during the night. The Emperor sighed wearily, "Don't they understand my true intentions yet?" he asked. He told Toda to assemble the Palace Guard. "I will talk to them myself," he said, intending to shatter still another precedent.

As matters turned out, Hirohito did not have to address his guards. On his way to summon them, another chamberlain met General Tanaka, who had come personally to rescind Hatanaka's forged orders and disband the rebellion. "Why do you tremble?" Tanaka asked the man. "The revolt is over. Everything is all right now." Tanaka was as good as his word: Within an hour, he had sent the guards back to their barracks and restored order.

Their heads bowed, some of them weeping, citizens in a Tokyo suburb hear the Emperor's voice for the first time in a radio broadcast announcing Japan's surrender. For days afterward, a journalist wrote, "people carried on their pursuits in a daze."

On Guam, which was recaptured by the United States in the summer of 1944, Japanese prisoners of war stand at attention, their eyes cast down, during a broadcast of Hirohito's five-minute-long capitulation speech.

At 11 o'clock that morning, Hatanaka played out his rebellion to its inevitable conclusion. On the wide plaza facing the Imperial Palace, the 33-year-old major and a fellow rebel passed out crudely printed leaflets imploring the people to rise up and prevent the forthcoming surrender. Nobody seemed much interested, and a few minutes later Hatanaka put a bullet through his forehead with the pistol he had used to assassinate General Mori. At the same time, his companion performed the rite of seppuku with a dagger, then shot himself.

At noon, activity all over Japan came to a halt. In factories, schools, homes and military bases, people gathered around loudspeakers and radios to listen to what an earlier newscast had promised would be an important broadcast. In Nagasaki's Urakami valley, a crowd gathered around a loudspeaker that had been set up in a schoolyard within sight of a mound of blackened corpses. In Hiroshima, people stood before a loudspeaker that had been placed outside one of the city's demolished railway stations. In Tokyo, Hirohito himself sat before an old RCA radio outside the underground conference room. The first voice the Emperor and his subjects heard was that of Chokugen Wada, a well-known announcer. "This will be a broadcast of the gravest importance," Wada intoned nervously. "Will all listeners please rise. His Majesty the Emperor will now read his Imperial Rescript to the people of Japan. We respectfully transmit his voice."

The national anthem, "Kimigayo," was played, and then, for the first time in history, the Emperor spoke to the people of Japan:

"The enemy has begun to employ a new and most cruel bomb. Should we continue to fight, it would not only result in an ultimate collapse and obliteration of the Japanese nation, but also it would lead to the total extinction of human civilization. This is the reason why We have or-

dered the acceptance of the provisions of the Joint Declaration of the Powers.

"Let the entire nation continue as one family from generation to generation. Unite your total strength to be devoted to the construction of the future. Cultivate the ways of rectitude, foster nobility of spirit, and work with resolution that you may enhance the innate glory of the Imperial State and keep pace with the progress of the world."

Millions of Japanese wept at the Emperor's words—their tears a mixture of grief and humiliation for what had been lost and relief that their long suffering was over. In Tokyo, hundreds of people crowded in front of the Imperial Palace to bow to the Emperor. Periodically, their keening was punctuated by pistol shots as Army and Navy officers committed suicide in their midst.

In Nagasaki, the distant drone of enemy reconnaissance planes—circling overhead to photograph the aftereffects of the second atomic bomb—provided a strange counterpoint to the bitter weeping below. In many places, people did not know what to make of the Emperor's announcement. Many believed the War was over because Japan had won. "We thought there was no other way the War could end," recalled a man who had been a member of the crowd at the Hiroshima station.

Some Japanese soldiers refused to lay down their arms, and some engaged in a final act of barbarism. In Fukuoka, 100 miles north of Nagasaki, officers at the Western Army headquarters hacked 16 captured American fliers to death with their swords. And at Oita Field on Kyushu, Vice Admiral Matome Ugaki, commander of the Navy's Fifth Air Fleet, planned his own suicide—a last attack on the enemy.

At 5 o'clock that afternoon, Admiral Ugaki, carrying his samurai sword and wearing a uniform stripped of all insignia and braid, walked toward the runway. There he found 11 fighter-bombers ready for takeoff, their two-man crews standing alongside them.

Ugaki was dumfounded. "Are you so willing to die with me?" he asked. The 22 men responded by raising their hands in salute. When Ugaki took his seat behind the pilot of the lead plane, a warrant officer clambered up beside him, protesting, "You have taken my place." Ugaki smiled. "I have relieved you," he said. The enlisted man, for once unawed by rank, tried to squeeze in beside him. Obligingly, the Admiral moved over.

At 7:24 p.m., Ugaki radioed his base. "I am going to make an attack on Okinawa, where my men have fallen like cherry blossoms," he declared. A few minutes later, he sent a final message that his formation had gone into an attack-

Vice Admiral Matome Ugaki, commander of the Imperial Navy's Fifth Air Fleet, stands ready on August 15 to lead a squadron of dive bombers on a last suicide mission in defiance of the peace declaration that day. The Kamikazes attacked American ships north of Okinawa but crashed without inflicting any damage.

In the Oval Office, President Truman informs reporters of Japan's surrender. Seated behind him are Admiral William D. Leahy and Secretary of State James F. Byrnes. Afterward, Truman telephoned his mother in Missouri to tell her the War was over.

ing dive. That was the last anyone heard of Admiral Ugaki and his suicide squadron.

Years later, an American sailor named Danny Rosewell solved the mystery of Ugaki's last moments when he revealed to a Japanese historian that he had seen several Kamikazes attacking off Iheya-ushiro-jima, north of Okinawa. One of the planes, trailing smoke and flames, crashed on the beach. The next morning, Rosewell inspected the plane and found three bodies in the two-seated aircraft. One of the men had an ornate samurai sword. It was Ugaki.

Less than 24 hours after Emperor Hirohito's momentous broadcast to his people, reporters in Washington crowded into the Oval Office of the White House to hear President Truman announce: "I have just received a note from the Japanese government in reply to the message forwarded to that government by the Secretary of State on August 11. I deem this reply a full acceptance of the Potsdam Declaration, which specifies the unconditional surrender of Japan." It was 7 p.m. on August 15, 1945.

On Guam, Captain Edwin T. Layton walked into the office of his boss, Admiral Chester W. Nimitz, commander of American forces in the Pacific, with news of the Japanese surrender. Nimitz, Layton later recalled, "didn't get jubilant or jump up and down like I saw some other officers do. He merely smiled in his own calm way."

The news reached Admiral William F. Halsey, commander of the Third Fleet, on his flagship, the battleship *Missouri,* off the coast of Japan. Halsey's reaction was markedly different from that of Nimitz. He let out a loud "Yippee!" and pounded every shoulder within reach. When he had calmed down, he ordered the flags for "well done" hoisted, and then just to be on the safe side, he issued an order to his carrier pilots to "investigate and shoot down all snoopers—not vindictively, but in a friendly sort of way."

Spontaneous celebrations erupted throughout Halsey's fleet. Crewmen danced and hugged each other on deck to the accompaniment of the shrill music of hundreds of whistles. "Every ship broke out its largest ensign," said one officer, "and the men vied with one another to see who could yell the loudest."

A large force of American fighters and bombers was approaching Tokyo when it was notified to jettison all bombs and return to base. One pilot was puzzled by Halsey's contradictory instructions. "What does the Admiral mean, 'not vindictively'?" he queried his wingman. The reply was instantaneous: "I think he means for us to use only three guns instead of six." Indeed, the shooting was not

quite over. At 11:25 that morning, a Japanese pilot defiantly attacked Halsey's fleet. Navy gunners easily shot down the lone pilot, as well as four others who followed, and American fliers—taking the Admiral at his word—brought down an additional 38 Japanese aircraft on the last day of hostilities.

In Tokyo the Cabinet resigned en masse after Hirohito's broadcast, and Prime Minister Suzuki was succeeded by Prince Higashikuni, an uncle of the Emperor. The new Prime Minister did not possess striking intellectual talents, but he had two attributes that made him the ideal person to lead Japan through the crucial days just ahead: his blood link to the throne, which would reassure the people of the continuance of the imperial line, and his experience as a general, which made him acceptable to the military.

Events moved rapidly. Shortly after Suzuki's Cabinet resigned, General Douglas MacArthur, commander of American ground forces in the Pacific, radioed Tokyo that the Allies had accepted its surrender offer and ordered the Japanese to send a delegation to the Philippines. MacArthur, wary of continued Japanese resistance, told Tokyo its delegation was to bring with it all of Japan's defense plans. In turn, the Americans would spell out terms of the forthcoming occupation.

The idea of such a mission was almost too humiliating for proud Japanese officers to swallow. General Umezu, the Army Chief of Staff, refused to participate and insisted that his deputy, General Torashiro Kawabe, go in his stead. Kawabe had trouble finding men for the mission but eventually persuaded 15 officers and diplomats to accompany him to Manila.

Early on the morning of August 19, Kawabe's delegation boarded two Mitsubishi bombers in Tokyo. On Allied instructions, the two planes—known to the Americans as Bettys—had been painted white with large green crosses on the sides of their fuselages. Twelve hours later, after having transferred to an American C-54 transport on Ie-jima, Kawabe's delegation arrived in Manila.

The Japanese stepped off the plane at Nichols Field to a scene that bordered on pandemonium. Thousands of cat-calling soldiers and civilians pressed in on them as they were escorted to waiting cars. To one delegate, the frantic clicking of cameras was like "machine guns fired at strange animals." As the procession passed through Manila, thou-

sands of Filipinos—remembering the years of occupation and the havoc the Japanese had wreaked when they abandoned the city the previous February—cursed and shouted; some threw stones at the cars.

That evening, the Japanese delegates were taken to City Hall for their first meeting with their American counterparts. After giving up their swords at the entrance, they were escorted to a second-floor conference room. Awaiting them was MacArthur's Chief of Staff, Lieut. General Richard K. Sutherland Jr., a tough officer who had been heard to say "Someone's got to be the bastard around here." MacArthur himself refused to see the Japanese until the moment when they actually surrendered.

In a voice that brooked no argument, Sutherland read General Order Number One: Japanese forces in Manchuria and northern Korea would capitulate to the Russians, while units in Indochina, Formosa and China would surrender to the Chinese. All other Japanese combatants would surrender to the Americans and the British.

Kawabe listened stoically as Sutherland laid down the terms of Japan's capitulation. But when the American told him that United States forces would begin landing at Tokyo's Atsugi Air Base on August 23, four days hence, Kawabe's composure broke. "The Japanese side would sincerely advise you not to land so quickly," he protested. "You should know that we are still having trouble at home with some of the Kamikaze units. At least 10 days are needed to prepare." Sutherland ignored Kawabe's protest. MacArthur himself would land at Atsugi on August 26, he said, and receive the Japanese surrender two days later.

Sutherland then told the Japanese to begin giving his team details of their military strength. Through most of the night, they revealed the remaining secrets of their shattered Empire, including the positions of all Army and Navy units, ammunition dumps, coastal guns and minefields. Sutherland was especially eager to know the location of all *kaitens,* the deadly human torpedoes that he feared diehards might use against American troop landings.

By 4 a.m., Kawabe's delegation had finished its painful task. Sutherland was pleased with the Japanese cooperation and made his first concession as he closed the meeting: "The Japanese side has furnished all necessary information, and is very eager to have a peaceful occupation without any

trouble. We do not want any wasted time, but we will make the landing date August 28."

At 1 p.m., the C-54 transport carrying the Japanese delegation took off for Ie-jima. In 19 hours, the two sides had made a good beginning toward disengagement.

Shortly after dawn on the 28th of August, 45 American C-47 transports landed at Atsugi Air Base, and the Occupation of Japan began *(pages 188-201).* The American battleships *Missouri* and *South Dakota* and the British battleship *Duke of York* anchored in Tokyo Bay the following day along with hundreds of other warships. The stage was set for the arrival of Admiral Nimitz and General MacArthur, the Pacific theater's five-star commanders.

When Nimitz arrived by flying boat on the afternoon of August 29, he was seething over President Truman's recent selection of MacArthur to conduct the surrender ceremonies and oversee the Occupation. Nimitz had no desire to command the Occupation, but he was openly annoyed that the Army was about to take the spotlight in a war whose brunt he felt the Navy had borne. In Washington, Secretary of the Navy Forrestal came to the rescue by suggesting that the surrender ceremony take place aboard the battleship *Missouri*—named for Truman's home state and christened in 1944 by his daughter, Margaret. Nimitz was delighted at Forrestal's suggestion, which President Truman was quick to approve.

By August 30, more than 4,000 troops of the 11th Airborne Division had landed at Atsugi. They were just in time to greet MacArthur, whose personal C-54, the *Bataan,* touched down at 2:19 p.m. The door of the plane opened, and the general, with his familiar corncob pipe clenched jauntily between his teeth, stood silently at the top of the landing ramp, savoring the moment. Smiling, MacArthur walked down the landing ramp, where General Robert Eichelberger, commander of the Eighth Army, was waiting for him. "Bob," MacArthur said simply, "this is the payoff."

The following day, an unexpected visitor added to MacArthur's elation. MacArthur was eating dinner in the Yokohama hotel where he had established temporary headquarters when an aide told him that Lieut. General Jonathan M. Wainwright had arrived. MacArthur rushed to embrace his old comrade, who had just been released

Assigned to meet the Japanese delegation summoned to Manila to arrange the surrender, Colonel Sidney Mashbir makes a point of refusing the proffered hand of Lieut. General Torashiro Kawabe, whom Mashbir had known before the War.

Residents of Kazo-machi line the town's main street for the farewell parade of the 5th Tank Regiment shortly before the unit's demobilization.

A RAPID FAREWELL TO ARMS

Even before the Americans arrived, Japan began to demobilize. War plants needed to be shut down; planes and ships as well as shore batteries had to be disarmed. For days, great clouds of black smoke rose from behind the War Ministry as staff officers burned their records.

Japan's fighting men, after poignant last parades, turned in their weapons at special collection centers and returned to their families. By the end of August, 1.5 million fighting men had become civilians again. "I know of no demobilization in history," observed General Douglas MacArthur, "accomplished so rapidly and so frictionlessly."

A returning soldier salutes farm workers and children.

from a prisoner-of-war camp in Manchuria. MacArthur was stunned at his friend's condition: Wainwright's hair had turned completely white, his uniform hung loosely on his emaciated frame and he needed a cane to stand erect. Wainwright feared that he was in disgrace for having surrendered the Philippines in 1942, but MacArthur assured him that he would be welcomed home as a hero. "Your old corps is yours whenever you want it," MacArthur promised, and he invited Wainwright to join him at the surrender ceremony two days hence.

At 7 a.m. on September 2, hundreds of newsmen from more than a score of countries arrived by destroyer to take up their assigned positions on the *Missouri*. They climbed on board in time to witness a color guard run the Stars and Stripes up the mainmast—the same flag that had been flying above the Capitol in Washington on December 7, 1941. Mounted on a nearby bulkhead was a second American flag, a tattered one with only 34 stars. It was the banner that Commodore Matthew Perry had flown aboard his flagship, the *Powhatan,* when he entered Tokyo Bay in 1854 to open Japan to the West. Halsey had ordered Perry's ensign rushed from the Naval Academy Museum for the surrender ceremony.

Just after 8 o'clock, Admiral Nimitz arrived on a motor barge from the *South Dakota.* After a short wait, the destroyer *Nichols* pulled alongside the *Missouri* and General MacArthur came aboard. He surveyed the panoply of brass before him, shook hands with Nimitz and Halsey and said, "It's grand to have so many of my colleagues from the shoestring days here at the end of the road." Conspicuous by his absence was Admiral Raymond Spruance, the much-decorated commander of the Fifth Fleet. Spruance was waiting off Okinawa on his flagship, the *New Jersey,* because Nimitz wanted someone ready to take command in the Pacific should Japanese fanatics attack the *Missouri.*

Once MacArthur was on board, the destroyer *Lands-downe* brought the Japanese delegation alongside.

At 8:55, Mamoru Shigemitsu, Japan's new Foreign Minister, made his way painfully up a gangway. Shigemitsu had lost his left leg to an assassin's bomb years earlier in Shanghai, and the artificial leg he wore caused him great distress as he climbed aboard the *Missouri*. Shigemitsu was followed by General Umezu.

Thousands of American sailors, soldiers and newsmen watched intently as the other nine members of the Japanese delegation came aboard and walked in front of a battered felt-covered mess table on which the surrender documents had been placed. "We waited a few minutes, standing in the public gaze like penitent schoolboys awaiting the dreaded schoolmaster," recalled Toshikazu Kase, a member of the delegation. "A million eyes seemed to beat on us like arrows barbed with fire. I felt them sink into my body with a sharp physical pain."

Lieut. General Sir Arthur Percival, recently freed from a prison camp in Manchuria, locked eyes momentarily with Colonel Ichiji Sugita, who had translated for Percival when he surrendered Singapore to the Japanese in 1942. Another delegate, Admiral Sadatoshi Tomioka, stared intently at Nimitz; for years the Japanese Navy's operations officer had kept Nimitz' picture in his office in an attempt to divine his rival's thinking. Always, he had failed.

MacArthur took his place behind the mess table and faced the Japanese. "We are gathered here," he intoned, "representatives of the major warring powers, to conclude a solemn agreement whereby peace may be restored. The issues, involving divergent ideals and ideologies, have been determined on the battlefields and hence are not for our discussion or our debate.

"It is my earnest hope," continued the 65-year-old MacArthur, his hands shaking visibly, "indeed the hope of all

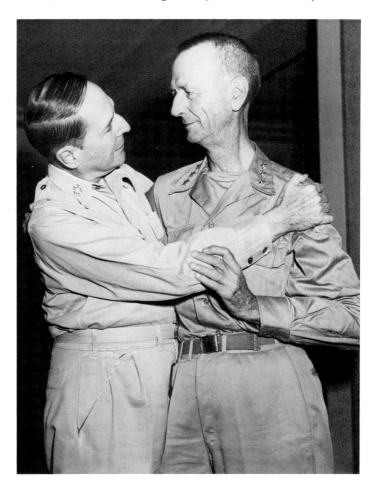

General MacArthur embraces an emaciated Lieut. General Jonathan M. Wainwright on his return from a Japanese POW camp in Manchuria. Wainwright, imprisoned since the fall of the Philippines in 1942, was flown to Tokyo to witness Japan's surrender.

mankind, that from this solemn occasion a better world shall emerge out of the blood and carnage of the past. As Supreme Commander of the Allied powers, it is my firm intention to discharge my responsibilities with justice and tolerance, while taking all necessary dispositions to insure that the terms of the surrender are fully, promptly and faithfully complied with."

MacArthur stepped back and motioned for Shigemitsu to sign the surrender document. The diplomat limped forward and sat at the table. Slowly, he removed his yellow gloves and silk top hat, placed them on the table, and for several moments stared at the paper before him.

"Show him where to sign," MacArthur said to General Sutherland, who stepped forward and pointed out the correct line. The Foreign Minister signed his name. Disdaining to sit, General Umezu marched forward, quickly slashed his signature across the document and walked stiffly back to the Japanese delegation.

Now it was General MacArthur's turn to sign for the Allies. Using three pens, he wrote his name a few letters at a time. He handed the first pen to General Wainwright, who had been near his side throughout the ceremony; General Percival got the second pen. MacArthur finished and put the last pen, a bright red one, into his pocket to take to his wife and son back in Manila.

Admiral Nimitz signed for the United States, and representatives of the other Allied nations added their names to the document. "Let us pray that peace be now restored to the world and that God will preserve it always," MacArthur intoned. "These proceedings are closed."

As the Japanese were led away, MacArthur put his arm around Halsey and asked, "Bill, where the hell are those airplanes?" Overhead, as if on cue, the sun came out for the first time that day, illuminating the peak of Mount Fuji and sparkling off the fuselages of 1,900 Allied planes that flew by in massive salute. The greatest tragedy in mankind's history, one that had claimed 55 million military and civilian casualties and consumed untold material wealth, was finally ended. After six years, the guns were silent.

Officers representing the Allied nations face the Japanese delegation across a

table on the battleship Missouri on September 2, 1945. General MacArthur (at microphone) watches General Yoshijiro Umezu sign the surrender document.

THE DAY THE WAR ENDED

Celebrating V-J Day far from home, U.S. servicemen and servicewomen in Paris display copies of the newspaper Stars and Stripes proclaiming "peace."

CELEBRATIONS OF TRIUMPH AND RELIEF

The revelry began hours before and continued for days after President Truman's brief formal announcement at 7 p.m. Eastern War Time on Tuesday, August 14, 1945: Japan had surrendered. The war in the Pacific was over, and people everywhere burst out in triumph and relief.

Americans celebrated the longest and loudest of all, for the nation had been steeling itself to launch an all-out invasion of Japan. Something like five million soldiers, sailors and airmen had been slated to participate in that fearsome battle, and the projected casualties were high. From New York to San Francisco, and in every town between, people rushed into the streets to give thanks and to hail the end of a time of shortages and sacrifice they had come to call "the duration." Men and women embraced, strangers became instant friends.

Delirium reigned among the servicemen rushing to join the celebration from their Army camps and airfields, Navy bases and Marine barracks. The barriers of rank dissolved in the realization that almost all of them would soon be civilians again. The GIs laughed and cheered and set out to kiss or be kissed by every girl in sight.

In a few places, the extended rejoicing got out of hand, and instances of violence and property damage resulted. But mostly it was a grand and glorious fete. At Pearl Harbor, which had become the symbol of America's wartime determination, the good news came at 3 a.m. and caught most people asleep. Soon, however, Honolulu rocked with noise and the night sky blazed with pyrotechnics as every ship in the harbor expended its store of rockets and flares.

If, among the victors, there was a touch of remorse over the terrible means by which the War had been shortened, it was not immediately apparent. What mattered for the moment was that peace had come at last and that there would be no more killing. At Los Alamos, scientists of the Manhattan Project tipsily loaded a jeep with 50-pound blocks of high explosives, lined up the blocks—21 of them—in a nearby canyon, and detonated the lot in a thunderous victory salute.

A crossed-out Rising Sun on the cover of the August 20, 1945, issue of Time wordlessly symbolizes victory over Japan and the end of the War.

Passersby in Times Square grin as a jubilant sailor locks nurse Edith Shain in a victory embrace on what one GI called "the kissingest day in history."

A conga line of soldiers, sailors and civilians weaves happily through Lafayette Park, opposite the White House, on August 14 as Washington awaits official word of the War's end.

A double chain of military police bends under the pressure of celebrants surging toward the White House fence moments after President Truman announced the Japanese acceptance of Allied surrender terms. Chants of "We want Harry!" brought the President and Mrs. Truman onto the lawn to share in the celebration.

Two million people inundate Times Square in New York City's biggest celebration ever. Their "victory roar," said one observer, "numbed the senses."

NEW YORK CITY

On Manhattan's Broadway, a sailor and a member of the Women's Army Corps exchange hats and dance a "victory jive."

New York merrymakers hoist a young woman with "V-J Day" painted in lipstick on her forehead. Some celebrations continued for three days, until military authorities ordered all service personnel back to their bases.

Crowds in San Francisco halt traffic on Market Street. Sadly, later that night some drunken servicemen went on a rampage, assaulting women and looting stores.

On Chicago's South Side, a block party forms around a bonfire of signs and V-J Day newspapers.

Swept off her feet, a Kansas City celebrant plants a kiss on Staff Sergeant Sam Kennedy, who was passing through the city. Some servicemen shredded their uniforms and gave away the tattered remains as souvenirs.

In occupied Berlin, a jeepload of American, British and Soviet soldiers wave their caps in the air to salute the final Allied victory.

American GIs and Navy officers in Paris cluster around a celebrating couple who hold a newspaper proclaiming Japan's capitulation.

In Chungking, joy lights the faces of Chinese celebrants, whose war with Japan began in 1937.

Bouncing high over Piccadilly Circus from a blanket pulled by dozens of willing hands, a London woman exemplifies the spirit of Britain's all-night celebration.

Searchlights, rockets and flares streak the night sky over Pearl Harbor as the U.S. Pacific Fleet celebrates the end of the war with Japan at the place where it

began. For Americans, the War had lasted three years, eight months and seven days and had claimed the lives of 292,131 servicemen and servicewomen.

A BLOODLESS INVASION

The sun sets behind Mount Fuji as ships of the U.S. Pacific Fleet ride at anchor near Tokyo on August 29, 1945, one day after the first Americans landed in Japan.

TENSE MEETING OF VICTOR AND VANQUISHED

The Japanese met the first conquerors in their history on August 28, 1945, when Colonel Charles Tench of the U.S. Army stepped from a C-47 transport onto the Tarmac at Atsugi air base, 30 miles southwest of Tokyo. Tench was understandably nervous, and the first thing he saw was not reassuring: Japanese soldiers were charging across the airstrip toward him. Tench fingered his .45-caliber pistol. Then he realized what had happened. The official reception committee and honor guard had been waiting at the far end of the runway and were aghast at having missed his landing.

Tench arrived in the lead plane of a fleet of 45 C-47s carrying supplies and 146 American soldiers—the advance contingent of nearly half a million Yanks who would land during the next month. The soldiers' immediate task was to secure Atsugi and make ready for the arrival two days later of General Douglas MacArthur, Supreme Commander for the Allied Powers. Tench's party had approached the mission with considerable trepidation. The betting back in Manila had been that the Americans would be shot on arrival. MacArthur tried to reassure his men, noting that Emperor Hirohito had ordered his people to lay down their arms, "and he is divine." But at least one officer wondered aloud how much force the Emperor's order would carry, since Japan had lost and "divinities aren't supposed to lose wars."

Even the Japanese feared trouble. Government officials had urged that the American landing be put off: Japan was not yet reconciled to surrender. Atsugi in particular, as a Kamikaze base, was a hotbed of hatred for the enemy. Even as the Japanese commander worked late at night to prepare for the Americans, two of his men dueled with swords outside his window over whether to continue the War.

As it turned out, the tense early hours of Occupation passed almost without a hitch. The Americans angered some Japanese commanders by disregarding protocol to rush supplies and medical aid to Allied prisoners of war—the only people in Japan who welcomed the conquerors with cheers. Yet, miraculously, no casualties were suffered, no shots fired in anger, as the troops flooded in.

In a cordial visit reflecting the tone of the U.S. Occupation, Emperor Hirohito calls on General Douglas MacArthur at the American Embassy.

Exultant Allied prisoners of war at a camp near Yokohama wave Dutch, American and British flags as their liberators approach on the 29th of August.

"NOBODY BUT A KAMIKAZE WOULD DARE LAND HERE"

As Colonel Tench and his advance party flew to Atsugi, one man noticed that the snow was gone from Mount Fuji's fabled slopes—and wondered, only half in jest, whether the Japanese had melted it all as a last gesture of defiance.

In fact, Lieut. General Seizo Arisue, who met the Americans, wanted to melt only tension. He offered Tench some punch, which Tench turned down, fearing poison. When Arisue drank some himself, Tench accepted the offer. Then the talks began.

On the airfield, 4,000 Japanese worked at repairing runways so scarred by bombs that one American muttered: "Nobody but a Kamikaze would dare land on this strip." Despite the craters, over the next two days scores of transports and 200 B-29s landed, the bombers touching down every two minutes in an impressive show of strength. One C-54—with *Bataan* painted on its nose—brought the Occupation's Supreme Commander, Douglas MacArthur.

Colonel Charles Tench and Lieut. General Seizo Arisue confer through interpreters at Atsugi air base.

Teen-age trainees from the Japanese Navy work to level the crushed-stone taxiway at Atsugi in order to make it ready for use by heavy American aircraft.

After deplaning at Atsugi, troops of the 188th Parachute Infantry Regiment move out in commandeered Japanese trucks to secure Yokohama, 15 miles away.

The 3rd Airdrome Squadron claims bragging rights—"First in Tokyo."

MacArthur's arrival in Japan recalls his earlier return to the Philippines.

Crowded on the deck of a transport vessel at the entrance to Tokyo Bay, troops from the U.S. 4th Marine Regiment are briefed on their imminent landing.

HITTING THE BEACH FOR A LAST TIME

By August 29, Tokyo Bay was crowded with one of the greatest armadas that had ever been brought together—258 battleships, cruisers, destroyers and other vessels of the U.S. Pacific Fleet, and a sampling of ships from other Allied countries. Every heavy gun in the fleet was directed toward the Japanese shore.

The next morning, 10,000 U.S. and 450 British Marines and sailors made a symbolic landing at the Yokosuka naval and air bases that guarded the bay's entrance. Fittingly, the first amphibious unit to touch Japanese soil was the 6th Marine Division's reborn 4th Regiment; the regiment had been wiped out in 1942 defending Bataan and Corregidor.

Combat-ready Marines race ashore at Yokosuka on August 30 to occupy the base and its airfield.

Five hundred yards inland, Marines encounter their first Japanese, who salute as they march forward to surrender.

Following the landing, American Marines inspect a Japanese coastal defense battery on Tokyo Bay—its guns now depressed in a symbol of surrender.

CALMING FEARS WITH COURTESY

The Japanese, too, feared their first encounters with the enemy. Officers carried suicide pistols with single bullets. Children were told that the Americans were monsters who "would squeeze our throats and kill us and make holes in our ears and string wires through them." Newspapers warned women to seek refuge in the hills.

Most Japanese just withdrew into their homes, or into a personal trance. Fleet Admiral Chester Nimitz noted that the Japanese police "act as if we were not in sight. They are not sullen or amazed, as one might expect. They simply do not see us."

American restraint and patience helped calm Japanese fears and end the spiritual withdrawal. MacArthur decreed that a GI who so much as slapped a Japanese would get five years in prison; rapists faced the death penalty. He let Japan's police force keep its side arms and allowed the Army to disarm itself. The GIs impressed the Japanese through everyday courtesies, like giving up their seats to elderly women—something the Japanese did only for members of their own families.

As a sign of deference—and to watch for snipers—a Japanese soldier guarding the road to Yokohama faces away from the passing American cavalcade.

Their faces averted, Japanese soldiers and civilians pass a U.S. Marine convoy rolling through a village outside Yokosuka.

His eyes on the ground, a Japanese policeman walks between lines of U.S. Marines as he leaves his village station.

As the Occupation begins, U.S. Marines in amphibious vehicles look over a rainy Japanese street scene at a staging depot in Saga, a port in southern Japan.

Alone on guard duty at a railroad station in Sasebo, a U.S. Marine in combat gear stands in contrast to Japanese on their way home after demobilization.

BIBLIOGRAPHY

Angelucci, Enzo, *The Rand McNally Encyclopedia of Military Aircraft: 1914-1980.* Transl. by S. M. Harris. Rand McNally, 1981.

Badash, Lawrence, Joseph O. Hirschfelder and Herbert P. Broida, eds., *Reminiscences of Los Alamos: 1943-1945.* D. Reidel Publishing, 1980.

Bainbridge, K. T., *Trinity.* Los Alamos Scientific Laboratory of the University of California, May 1976.

"The Berlin Conference." *Life,* August 6, 1945.

Blumberg, Stanley A., and Gwinn Owens, *Energy and Conflict: The Life and Times of Edward Teller.* G. P. Putnam's Sons, 1976.

Brown, Anthony Cave, and Charles B. MacDonald, eds., *The Secret History of the Atomic Bomb.* The Dial Press/James Wade, 1977.

Butow, Robert J. C., *Japan's Decision to Surrender.* Stanford University Press, 1954.

Chinnock, Frank W., *Nagasaki: The Forgotten Bomb.* The World Publishing Company, 1969.

The Committee for the Compilation of Material on Damage Caused by the Atomic Bombs in Hiroshima and Nagasaki, *Hiroshima and Nagasaki: The Physical, Medical and Social Effects of the Atomic Bombings.* Transl. by Eisei Ishikawa and David L. Swain. Basic Books, 1981.

Coox, Alvin, *Japan: The Final Agony.* Ballantine Books, 1970.

Costello, John, *The Pacific War.* Rawson, Wade Publishers, 1981.

Craig, William, *The Fall of Japan.* Penguin Books, 1967.

Craven, Wesley Frank, and James Lea Cate, eds., *The Army Air Forces in World War II,* Vol. 5, *The Pacific: Matterhorn to Nagasaki, June 1944 to August 1945.* The University of Chicago Press, 1953.

Cries for Peace: Experiences of Japanese Victims of World War II. Compiled by the Youth Division of Soka Gakkai. Tokyo: The Japan Times, 1978.

Current Biography: 1942. H. W. Wilson Company, 1942.

Current Biography: 1945. H. W. Wilson Company, 1945.

Days to Remember: An Account of the Bombings of Hiroshima and Nagasaki. Tokyo: Hiroshima-Nagasaki Publishing Committee, 1981.

Donovan, Robert J., *Conflict and Crisis: The Presidency of Harry S. Truman, 1945-1948.* W. W. Norton, 1977.

Ebener, Charlotte, *No Facilities for Women.* Alfred A. Knopf, 1955.

The Editors of Time-Life Books, *Japan at War* (World War II series). Time-Life Books, 1980.

Feis, Herbert, *The Atomic Bomb and the End of World War II.* Princeton University Press, 1966.

Ferrell, Robert H., ed., *Off the Record: The Private Papers of Harry S. Truman.* Harper & Row, 1980.

Francillon, René J., *Japanese Aircraft of the Pacific War.* London: Putnam, 1970.

Gallo, Max, *The Poster in History.* Transl. by Alfred and Bruni Mayor. American Heritage Publishing, 1974.

Goodchild, Peter, *J. Robert Oppenheimer: Shatterer of Worlds.* Houghton Mifflin, 1981.

Groueff, Stephane, *Manhattan Project: The Untold Story of the Making of the Atomic Bomb.* Little, Brown, 1967.

Groves, Leslie R., *Now It Can Be Told: The Story of the Manhattan Project.* Harper & Row, 1962.

Hachiya, Michihiko, *Hiroshima Diary: The Journal of a Japanese Physician, August 6-September 30, 1945.* Transl. and ed. by Warner Wells. The University of North Carolina Press, 1955.

Harriman, W. Averell, and Elie Abel, *Special Envoy to Churchill and Stalin: 1941-1946.* Random House, 1975.

Haynes, Richard F., *The Awesome Power.* Louisiana State University Press, 1973.

Hiroshima Genbaku Sanko Shiryo-Shu. Tokyo: Asahi Shimbunsha, 1968.

Hiroshima-Nagasaki: A Pictorial Record of the Atomic Destruction. Tokyo: Hiroshima-Nagasaki Publishing Committee, 1978.

History of the Second World War, No. 12, "Cult of the Kamikazes: A Japanese Pilot's First-hand Account." London: Purnell & Sons, 1967.

History of the Second World War, No. 15, "Hiroshima/Nagasaki." London: Purnell & Sons, 1967.

Hersey, John, *Hiroshima.* Bantam Books, 1946.

Ienaga, Saburo, ed., *Jugonen Senso,* Vol. 7, *Nihon no Rekiski.* Japan: Horupu Kyoiku Taikei, 1977.

Imai, Seiichi, *Taisen e no Michi,* Vol. 6, *Zusetsu Showa no Rekishi,* Tokyo: Shueisha, 1980.

"Japan Signs the Surrender." *Life,* September 17, 1945.

Japanese Broadcasting Corporation, *Unforgettable Fire: Pictures Drawn by Atomic Bomb Survivors.* Pantheon Books, 1977.

Jungk, Robert, *Brighter than a Thousand Suns: The Moral and Political History of the Atomic Scientists.* Transl. by James Cleugh. London: Victor Gollancz, 1958.

Karig, Walter, Russell L. Harris and Frank A. Manson, *Battle Report: Victory in the Pacific.* Rinehart and Company, 1949.

Kase, Toshikazu, *Journey to the Missouri.* Ed. by David Nelson Rowe. Archon Books, 1969.

Kato, Masuo, *The Lost War: A Japanese Reporter's Inside Story.* Alfred A. Knopf, 1946.

Kaufman, Louis, Barbara Fitzgerald and Tom Sewell, *Moe Berg: Athlete, Scholar, Spy.* Little, Brown, 1974.

Kilbourn, Jonathan:
"The Mighty Atom." *Yank, the Army Weekly,* September 7, 1945.
"The Atomic Bomb." *Yank, the Army Weekly,* September 7, 1945.

Kirby, S. Woodburn, *The War against Japan,* Vol. 5., *The Surrender of Japan.* London: Her Majesty's Stationery Office, 1969.

Kitajima, Muneto, *Gembaku no Nagasaki.* Tokyo: Gakufu Shoin, 1959.

Kosakai, Yoshiteru, compiler, *A-Bomb: A City Tells Its Story.* Transl. by Kiyoko Kageyama, Charlotte Susu-Mago and Kaoru Ogura. Hiroshima: Hiroshima Peace Culture Center, 1972.

Kunetka, James W., *City of Fire: Los Alamos and the Atomic Age, 1943-1945.* University of New Mexico Press, 1979.

Lamont, Lansing, *Day of Trinity.* Atheneum, 1965.

LeMay, Curtis E., with MacKinlay Kantor, *Mission with LeMay.* Doubleday, 1965.

Life, August 20, 1945.

Lifton, Robert Jay, *Death in Life.* Random House, 1967.

Los Alamos 1943-1945; the Beginning of an Era. Los Alamos Scientific Laboratory, no date.

Makino, Kikuo, ed., *Jugo no Senshi.* Tokyo: Mainichi Shimbunsha, 1980.

Manchester, William:
American Caesar: Douglas MacArthur, 1880-1964. Little, Brown, 1978.
The Glory and the Dream: A Narrative History of America, 1932-1972. Bantam Books, 1975.

Marx, Joseph Laurance:
Nagasaki: The Necessary Bomb? The Macmillan Company, 1971.
Seven Hours to Zero. G. P. Putnam's Sons, 1967.

Mee, Charles L., Jr., *Meeting at Potsdam.* Dell Publishing, 1976.

Meretskov, K. A., *Serving the People.* Transl. by David Fidlon. Moscow: Progress Publishers, 1971.

Mikesh, Robert C., "Kikka." *Monogram Close-Up 19.* Monogram Aviation Publications, 1979.

Miller, Merle, *Plain Speaking: An Oral Biography of Harry S. Truman.* Berkley Publishing, 1974.

Minasyan, M. M., et al., eds., *Great Patriotic War of the Soviet Union: 1941-1945.* Moscow: Progress Publishers, 1970.

Mitchell, Donald W., *A History of Russian and Soviet Sea Power.* Macmillan, 1974.

Moorad, George, *Lost Peace in China.* E. P. Dutton, 1949.

Morison, Samuel Eliot:
The Two-Ocean War: A Short History of the United States Navy in the Second World War. Little, Brown, 1963.
History of United States Naval Operations in World War II, Vol. 14, *Victory in the Pacific.* Little, Brown, 1975.

Moss, Michael E., *Posters for Victory: The American Home Front and World War II.* United States Military Academy, 1978.

Nishina, Kinen Zaidan, compiler, *Genshi-Bakidan: Hiroshima-Nagasaki no Shashin to Kiroku.* Tokyo: Kofusha Shoten, 1973.

The Pacific War Research Society:
The Day Man Lost: Hiroshima, 6 August 1945. Kodansha International, 1972.
Japan's Longest Day. Kodansha International, 1968.

Parrish, Thomas, ed., *The Simon and Schuster Encyclopedia of World War II.* Simon and Schuster, 1978.

"The People: Their Nation Is Beaten but They Are Not Bowed." *Life,* September 10, 1945.

Potter, E. B., *Nimitz.* Naval Institute Press, 1976.

Reports of General MacArthur: Japanese Operations in the Southwest Pacific Area. Vol. 2, Part II, compiled from Japanese Bureau Records. United States Government Printing Office, 1966.

Rhodes, Anthony Richard, *Propaganda, the Art of Persuasion: World War II.* Ed. by Victor Margolin. Chelsea House, 1976.

Rozental, S., ed., *Niels Bohr.* Amsterdam: North-Holland Publishing Company, 1967.

Schoenberger, Walter Smith, *Decision of Destiny.* Ohio University Press, 1969.

Schwartz, Robert, "Atomic Bomb Away." *Yank, the Army Weekly,* September 7, 1945.

Sherwin, Martin J., *A World Destroyed: The Atomic Bomb and the Grand Alliance.* Alfred A. Knopf, 1975.

The Staff of the *Mainichi Daily News, Fifty Years of Light and Dark: The Hirohito Era.* Tokyo: The Mainichi Newspapers, 1975.

Steichen, Edward, ed., *U.S. Navy War Photographs: Pearl Harbor to Tokyo Bay.* Crown Publishers, 1956.

Stephan, John J., *Sakhalin: A History.* London: Oxford University Press, 1971.

Suzuki, Tsutomu, ed., *Tai Heiyo,* Vol. 21, *Nihon Rekishi Shirizu.* Tokyo: Sekaibunkasha, 1968.

Takaoka, Susumu, "First Jet Flight in Japan." *Air B.P. No. 43.* October 1968.

Takeuchi, Shunzo, ed., *Dokyumento Tokyo Daikushu.* Tokyo: Ondorisha, 1968.

Thomas, Gordon, and Max Morgan Witts:
Enola Gay. Stein and Day, 1977.
Ruin from the Air: The Atomic Mission to Hiroshima. London: Hamish Hamilton, 1977.

Tibbets, Paul W., Jr., with Clair Stebbins and Harry Franken, *The Tibbets Story.* Stein and Day, 1978.

Time, August 20, 1945.

Time, August 27, 1945.

Togo, Shigenori, *The Cause of Japan.* Transl. and ed. by Togo Fumihiko and Ben Bruce Blakeney. Greenwood Press, 1977.

Toland, John, *The Rising Sun: The Decline and Fall of the Japanese Empire, 1936-1945.* Random House, 1970.

Truman, Harry S., *Memoirs.* 2 vols. Signet Books, 1965.

Truman, Margaret, *Harry S. Truman.* Pocket Books, 1974.

Turkin, Hy, and S. C. Thompson, *The Official Encyclopedia of Baseball.* A. S. Barnes, 1956.

The United States Strategic Bombing Survey, *The Effects of Atomic Bombs on Hiroshima and Nagasaki.* United States Government Printing Office, 1946.

"Victory." *Yank, The Army Weekly,* September 7, 1945.

"Victory Celebrations." *Life,* August 27, 1945.

"Victory! The Warsick World Hails It Wildly with Jap Broken by Shock of Cosmic Weapons." *Newsweek,* August 20, 1945.

Werth, Alexander, *Russia at War: 1941-1945.* E. P. Dutton, 1964.

Willoughby, Charles A., and John Chamberlain, *MacArthur: 1941-1951.* McGraw-Hill, 1954.

Yass, Marion, *Hiroshima.* G. P. Putnam's Sons, 1972.

Yui, Masaomi, *Senso to Kokumin,* Vol. 8, *Zusetsu Showa no Rekishi.* Tokyo: Shueisha, 1980.

ACKNOWLEDGMENTS

For help given in the preparation of this book, the editors wish to express their gratitude to Harold M. Agnew, General Atomic Company, San Diego, California; Captain C. Marriner Bertholf, USNR, Alexandria, Virginia; James Breen, Los Alamos National Laboratory, Los Alamos, New Mexico; Barbara Burger, Still Picture Branch, National Archives, Washington, D.C.; Richard Cannon, Williamsville, New York; Committee of Japanese Citizens to Send Gift Copies of a Photographic and Pictorial Record of the Atomic Bombing to Our Children and Fellow Human Beings of the World, Tokyo; Russel Gackenbach, West Caldwell, New Jersey; Arlin Givens, Los Alamos National Laboratory, Los Alamos, New Mexico; Phillip C. Guzzetta, M.D., Attending Surgeon, Children's Hospital, Washington, D.C.; Hiroshima Peace Memorial Museum, Hiroshima; Japan Broadcast Publishing Co., Tokyo; Robert Lewis, Smithfield, Virginia; Robert C. Mikesh, Curator of Aircraft, National Air and Space Museum, Washington, D.C.; Donald Montoya, White Sands Missile Range, White Sands, New Mexico; David Moore, Los Alamos National Laboratory, Los Alamos, New Mexico; Masao Murata, Tokyo; Nagasaki International Cultural Hall, Nagasaki; Charles Perry, Wrentham, Massachusetts; J. Simmonds, Imperial War Museum, London; Jim Trimble, National Archives, Washington, D.C.; Paul White, Audio-Visual Division, National Archives, Washington, D.C.

The index for this book was prepared by Nicholas J. Anthony.

PICTURE CREDITS

Credits from left to right are separated by semicolons, from top to bottom by dashes.

COVER and page 1: Mitsugu Kishida.

SPECTER OF A HALF-WON WAR—6-15: Henry Beville, courtesy the National Archives.

A RACE TO HARNESS THE ATOM—18: Map by Tarijy Elsab. 20: Fritz Goro for *Life*—Goro from Black Star. 21: UPI. 22, 23: U.S. Department of Energy. 24: Edward Clark for *Life*. 25: Argonne National Laboratory. 27: Edward Clark for *Life*. 29: Wide World. 30: U.S. Army. 31: Los Alamos National Laboratory. 33: U.S. Army.

COUNTDOWN IN THE DESERT—34, 35: Fritz Goro for *Life*. 36: Los Alamos National Laboratory. 37: Marie Hansen for *Life*. 38-52: Los Alamos National Laboratory—U.S. Army. 54, 55: Los Alamos National Laboratory. 56: U.S. Army—Los Alamos National Laboratory. 57: Fritz Goro for *Life*.

THE PRESIDENT'S ULTIMATUM—61: Dmitri Kessel for *Life*. 63: Samuel Berg, M.D. 64, 65: Art by John Batchelor, London. 66: David Irving, London. 67: Argonne National Laboratory. 68: U.S. Marine Corps. 69: *Yomiuri Shimbun*; from *Japan's Longest Day*, compiled by the Pacific War Research Society, published by Kodansha International Ltd., Tokyo, 1960. 70: Shunkichi Kikuchi. 71: *Mainichi Shimbun*—Shunkichi Kikuchi. 72: UPI.

THE MAN FROM MISSOURI—74, 75: Historical Pictures Service Inc., Chicago, courtesy The Harry S. Truman Library. 76: National Archives (No. 208-N-30470A). 77, 78: Courtesy The Harry S. Truman Library. 79: *The Kansas City Star-Times*, courtesy The Harry S. Truman Library—Edwin Saxton, courtesy The Harry S. Truman Library. 80: UPI, courtesy The Harry S. Truman Library. 81, 82: Courtesy The Harry S. Truman Library. 83, 84: UPI, courtesy The Harry S. Truman Library. 85: © Field Enterprises, courtesy The Harry S. Truman Library—*Life*, courtesy The Harry S. Truman Library. 86, 87: National Archives (No. 306-PS-50-13209); U.S. Army, courtesy The Harry S. Truman Library.

TARGET: HIROSHIMA—90: From the books *Enola Gay* and *Ruin from the Air*, by Gordon Thomas and Max Morgan Witts, published by Stein and Day, New York, and Hamish Hamilton, London, 1977. 91: Courtesy Jacob Beser. 92: U.S. Air Force. 93: Film from Defense Department files. 94: Courtesy Richard Cannon. 95: Courtesy Charles Perry. 96: Wide World. 97: U.S. Air Force. 98: National Archives (No. RG 77) (2); Frederic F. Bigio from B-C Graphics (2). 100: Wide World.

EYEWITNESS TO DOOMSDAY—102, 103: Painting by Sumako Yamada. 104: Painting by Sadako Kimura. 105: Painting by Goro Kiyoyoshi, courtesy Japan Broadcasting Publishing Co. 106: Painting by Kanichi Ito, courtesy Japan Broadcasting Publishing Co.—painting by Hatsuji Takeuchi. 107: Painting by Shouichi Furukawa—painting by Yoshiko Michitsuji, courtesy Japan Broadcasting Publish-

ing Co. 108: Painting by Akira Onoki—painting by Kazuo Matsumuro, courtesy Japan Broadcasting Publishing Co. 109: Painting by Asa Shigemori—painting by Zenko Ikeda and Chieko Ikeda. 110, 111: Painting by Masao Kobayashi; painting by Kinzo Nishida—painting by Kishiro Nagara. 112: Painting by Akiko Takakura—painting by Junjiro Wataoka, courtesy Japan Broadcasting Publishing Co. 113: Painting by Yasuko Yamagata—painting by Masato Yamashita, courtesy Japan Broadcasting Publishing Co. 114, 115: Painting by Kunito Terai—painting by Takeichi Yamaguchi; painting by Yoshimi Hara. 116, 117: Painting by Kiyoshi Wakai; painting by Tomiko Ikeshoji—painting by Kizo Kawakami. 118, 119: Painting by Hiroshi Matsuzoe; painting by Yoshito Nagamatsu.

SOME WHO ENDURED—122: Mitsuo Matsushige. 123: Yoshito Matsushige. 124: Kenichi Kimura. 125: Hajime Miyatake. 126: Satsuo Nakada. 127: Masami Onuka. 128, 129: Shigeo Hayashi. 130-132: Yosuke Yamabata. 133: Bottom, Kenichi Kimura. 134: FPG/Photoworld; Wide World.

ASSESSING THE AFTERMATH—136, 137: Yosuke Yamabata. 138: Yuichiro Sasaki. 139: Shigeo Hayashi. 140, 141: FPG/Photoworld; U.S. Air Force. 142, 143: Eiichi Matsumoto; U.S. Air Force (2). 144, 145: Shigeo Hayashi; Shunkichi Kikuchi. 146: U.S. Air Force—National Archives (No. 243-H-836). 147: Shigeo Hayashi. 148: Eiichi Matsumoto—U.S. Air Force. 149: Shigeo Hayashi. 150, 151: Hajime Miyatake.

BEARING THE UNBEARABLE—154: Keystone Press Ltd., London. 156: Bureau Soviétique d'Information, Paris. 157: Sovfoto—Bureau Soviétique d'Information, Paris. 158: Courtesy Masahiko Takeshita. 160: Ichiro Shirakawa. 161: *Yomiuri Shimbun*. 162: Courtesy Koremasa Anami. 164: *Mainichi Shimbun*. 165: National Archives (No. 80-G-490320). 166: Courtesy Mannosuke Toda. 167: Photo Trends. 168: George Lacks for *Life*. 170: Shigeyuke Kiyomatsu—*Mainichi Shimbun*. 171: U.S. Army. 172, 173: Carl Mydans for *Life*.

THE DAY THE WAR ENDED—174, 175: U.S. Army. 176: © 1945 Time Inc. 177: Alfred Eisenstaedt for *Life*. 178, 179: Wide World; UPI. 180: Herbert Gehr for *Life*. 181: Wide World—FPG/Photoworld. 182, 183: Wide World; Myron Davis for *Life*—Earl Hense from *The Kansas City Star-Times*. 184, 185: Ullstein Bilderdienst, Berlin (West)—U.S. Army; Keystone Press, Ltd., London; UPI. 186, 187: National Archives (No. 80-G-495604).

THE BLOODLESS INVASION—188, 189: U.S. Navy. 190: U.S. Army. 191: National Archives (No. 80-G-490444). 192, 193: U.S. Army except bottom right, Carl Mydans for *Life*. 194, 195: U.S. Marine Corps except bottom left, National Archives (No. 80-G-700860). 196, 197: Carl Mydans for *Life*; U.S. Marine Corps (2). 198-201: U.S. Marine Corps.